Harvard
Business
Review

ON
MEASURING
CORPORATE
PERFORMANCE

THE HARVARD BUSINESS REVIEW PAPERBACK SERIES

The series is designed to bring today's managers and professionals the fundamental information they need to stay competitive in a fast-moving world. From the preeminent thinkers whose work has defined an entire field to the rising stars who will redefine the way we think about business, here are the leading minds and landmark ideas that have established the *Harvard Business Review* as required reading for ambitious businesspeople in organizations around the globe.

Other books in the series:

Harvard Business Review on Change

Harvard Business Review on Knowledge Management

Harvard Business Review on Leadership

Harvard Business Review on Strategies for Growth

Harvard Business Review

ON

MEASURING CORPORATE PERFORMANCE

A HARVARD BUSINESS REVIEW PAPERBACK

Contents

Harvard Business Review

ON

MEASURING
CORPORATE
PERFORMANCE

The Information Executives Truly Need

PETER F. DRUCKER

Executive Summary

THE ABILITY TO GATHER, ARRANGE, AND MANIPULATE INFORMATION with computers has given business people new tools for managing. But data processing tools have done more than simply enable executives to do the same tasks better. They have changed the very concepts of what a business is and what managing means. To manage in the future, executives will need an information system integrated with strategy, rather than individual tools that so far have been used largely to record the past.

Many businesses have already shifted from traditional cost accounting to activity-based costing, which records the cost of the total process of providing a product or service. Activity-based costing integrates what were once several activities—value analysis, process analysis, quality management, and costing—into one

1

analysis. By using it, service and knowledge-based businesses can get cost information and yield control for the first time.

A company also must know the costs of its entire economic chain. It must work with all the other businesses that contribute to the final product, which will require compatible accounting systems and information sharing across companies. The shift from cost-led pricing to price-led costing, in which the price the customer is willing to pay determines allowable costs, will force companies into economic-chain costing.

The executive's tool kit has four kinds of diagnostic information: foundation information, productivity information, competence information, and resource-allocation information. The sources of the information are so diverse, and sifting through and interpreting it for a specific business are so difficult, that even small companies will need help from data specialists.

E VER SINCE THE NEW DATA PROCESSING TOOLS FIRST EMERGED 30 or 40 years ago, businesspeople have both overrated and underrated the importance of information in the organization. We—and I include myself—overrated the possibilities to the point where we talked of computer-generated "business models" that could make decisions and might even be able to run much of the business. But we also grossly underrated the new tools; we saw in them the means to do better what executives were already doing to manage their organizations.

Nobody talks of business models making economic decisions anymore. The greatest contribution of our data processing capacity so far has not even been to management. It has been to operations—for example, computer-assisted design or the marvelous software that architects now use to solve structural problems in the buildings they design.

Yet even as we both overestimated and underestimated the new tools, we failed to realize that they would drastically change the *tasks* to be tackled. Concepts and tools, history teaches again and again, are mutually interdependent and interactive. One changes the other. That is now happening to the concept we call a business and to the tools we call information. The new tools enable us—indeed, may force us—to see our businesses differently:

- as generators of resources, that is, as organizations that can convert business costs into yields;

- as links in an economic chain, which managers need to understand as a whole in order to manage their costs;

- as society's organs for the creation of wealth; and

- as both creatures and creators of a material environment, the area outside the organization in which opportunities and results lie but in which the threats to the success and the survival of every business also originate.

This article deals with the tools executives require to generate the information they need. And it deals with the concepts underlying those tools. Some of the tools have been around for a long time, but rarely, if ever, have they been focused on the task of managing a business. Some have to be refashioned; in their present form they no longer work. For some tools that promise to be important in the future, we have so far only the briefest specifications. The tools themselves still have to be designed.

Even though we are just beginning to understand how to use information as a tool, we can outline with high probability the major parts of the information system executives need to manage their businesses. So, in turn, can we begin to understand the concepts likely to underlie the business—call it the redesigned corporation—that executives will have to manage tomorrow.

From Cost Accounting to Yield Control

We may have gone furthest in redesigning both business and information in the most traditional of our information systems: accounting. In fact, many businesses have already shifted from traditional cost accounting to activity-based costing. *Activity-based costing* represents both a different concept of the business process, especially for manufacturers, and different ways of measuring.

Traditional cost accounting, first developed by General Motors 70 years ago, postulates that total manufacturing cost is the sum of the costs of individual operations. Yet the cost that matters for competitiveness and profitability is the cost of the total process, and that is what the new activity-based costing records and makes manageable. Its basic premise is that manufacturing is an integrated process that starts when supplies, materials, and parts arrive at the plant's loading dock and continues even after the finished product reaches the end user. Service is still a cost of the product, and so is installation, even if the customer pays.

Traditional cost accounting measures what it costs to *do* a task, for example, to cut a screw thread. Activity-based costing also records the cost of *not doing,* such as the cost of machine downtime, the cost of waiting for a needed part or tool, the cost of inventory waiting to be shipped, and the cost of reworking or scrapping a defective part. The costs of not doing, which traditional cost accounting cannot and does not record, often equal and sometimes even exceed the costs of doing. Activity-based costing therefore gives not only much better cost control, but increasingly, it also gives *result control.*

Traditional cost accounting assumes that a certain operation—for example, heat treating—has to be done and that it has to be done where it is being done now. Activity-based costing asks, Does it have to be done? If so, where is it best done? Activity-based costing integrates what were once several activities—value analysis, process analysis, quality management, and costing—into one analysis.

Using that approach, activity-based costing can substantially lower manufacturing costs—in some instances by a full third or more. Its greatest impact, however, is likely to be in services. In most manufacturing companies, cost accounting is inadequate. But service industries—banks, retail stores, hospitals, schools, newspapers, and radio and television stations—have practically no cost information at all.

Activity-based costing shows us why traditional cost accounting has not worked for service companies. It is not because the techniques are wrong. It is because traditional cost accounting makes the wrong assumptions. Service companies cannot start with the cost of individual operations, as manufacturing companies have done with traditional cost accounting. They must start with the assumption that there is only *one* cost: that of the total system. And it is a fixed cost over any given time period. The famous distinction between fixed and variable costs, on which traditional cost accounting is based, does not make much sense in services. Neither does the basic assumption of traditional cost accounting: that capital can be substituted for labor. In fact, in knowledge-based work especially, additional capital investment will likely require more, rather than less, labor. For example, a hospital that buys a new diagnostic tool may have to add four or five people to run it. Other knowledge-based organizations have had to learn the same lesson. But that all costs are fixed over a given time period and that resources cannot be substituted for one another, so that the *total* operation has to be costed—those are precisely the assumptions with which activity-based costing starts. By applying them to services, we are beginning for the first time to get cost information and yield control.

Banks, for instance, have been trying for several decades to apply conventional cost-accounting techniques to their business—that is, to figure the costs of individual operations and services—with almost negligible results. Now they are beginning to ask, Which one *activity* is at the center of costs and of results? The answer: serving the customer. The cost per customer in any major area of banking is a fixed cost. Thus it is the *yield* per customer—both the volume of services a customer uses and the mix of those services—that determines costs and profitability. Retail discounters, especially those in Western Europe, have known that for some time. They assume that once a unit of shelf space is installed, the cost is fixed and management consists of maximizing the yield thereon over a given time span. Their focus on yield control has enabled them to increase profitability despite their low prices and low margins.

Service businesses are only beginning to apply the new costing concepts. In some areas, such as research labs, where productivity is nearly impossible to measure, we may always have to rely on assessment and judgment rather than on measurement. But for most knowledge-based and service work, we should, within 10 to 15 years, have developed reliable tools to measure and manage costs and to relate those costs to results.

Thinking more clearly about costing in services should yield new insights into the costs of getting and keeping customers in all kinds of businesses. If GM, Ford, and Chrysler had used activity-based costing, for example, they would have realized early on the utter futility of their competitive blitzes of the past few years, which offered new-car buyers spectacular discounts and hefty cash rewards. Those promotions actually cost the Big Three automakers enormous amounts of money and, worse, enormous numbers of potential customers. In fact, every one resulted in a nasty drop in market standing. But neither the costs of the special deals nor their negative yields appeared in the companies' conventional cost-accounting figures, so management never saw the damage. Conventional cost accounting shows only the costs of individual manufacturing operations in isolation, and those were not affected by the discounts and rebates in the marketplace. Also, con-

If U.S. automakers had used activity-based costing, they would have realized the futility of their competitive blitzes.

ventional cost accounting does not show the impact of pricing decisions on such things as market share.

Activity-based costing shows—or at least attempts to show—the impact of changes in the costs and yields of every activity on the results of the whole. Had the automakers used it, it soon would have shown the damage done by the discount blitzes. In fact, because the Japanese already use a form of activity-based costing—though still a fairly primitive one—Toyota, Nissan, and Honda knew better than to compete with U.S. automakers through discounts and thus maintained both their market share and their profits.

From Legal Fiction to Economic Reality

Knowing the cost of your operations, however, is not enough. To succeed in the increasingly competitive global market, a company has to know the costs of its entire economic chain and has to work with other members of the chain to manage costs and maximize yield. Companies are therefore beginning to shift from costing only what goes on inside their own organizations to costing the entire economic process, in which even the biggest company is just one link.

The legal entity, the company, is a reality for shareholders, for creditors, for employees, and for tax collectors. But *economically,* it is fiction. Thirty years ago, the Coca-Cola Company was a franchisor. Independent bottlers manufactured the product. Now the company owns most of its bottling operations in the United States. But Coke drinkers—even those few who know that fact—could not care less. What matters in the marketplace is the economic reality, the costs of the entire process, regardless of who owns what.

Again and again in business history, an unknown company has come from nowhere and in a few short years overtaken the established leaders without apparently even breathing hard. The explanation always given is superior strategy, superior technology, superior marketing, or lean manufacturing. But in every single case, the newcomer also enjoys a tremendous cost advantage, usually about 30%. The reason is always the same: the new company knows and manages the costs of the entire economic chain rather than its costs alone.

What matters in the marketplace is the economic reality, the costs of the entire economic process, not who owns what.

Toyota is perhaps the best-publicized example of a company that knows and manages the costs of its suppliers and distributors; they are all, of course, members of its *keiretsu*. Through that network, Toyota manages the total cost of making, distributing, and servicing its cars as one cost stream, putting work where it costs the least and yields the most.

Managing the economic cost stream is not a Japanese invention, however, but a U.S. one. It began with the man who designed and built General Motors, William Durant. About 1908, Durant began to buy small, successful automobile companies—Buick, Oldsmobile, Cadillac, Chevrolet—and merged them into his new General Motors Corporation. In 1916, he set up a separate subsidiary called United Motors to buy small, successful parts companies. His first acquisitions included Delco, which held Charles Kettering's patents to the automotive self-starter.

Durant ultimately bought about 20 supplier companies; his last acquisition—in 1919, the year before he was

ousted as GM's CEO—was Fisher Body. Durant deliberately brought the parts and accessories makers into the
design process of a new automobile model right from
the start. Doing so allowed him to manage the total
costs of the finished car as one cost stream. In fact,
Durant invented the keiretsu.

However, between 1950 and 1960, Durant's keiretsu
became an albatross around the company's neck, as
unionization imposed higher labor costs on GM's parts
divisions than on their independent competitors. As the
outside customers, the independent automobile companies such as Packard and Studebaker, which had bought
50% of the output of GM's parts divisions, disappeared
one by one, GM's control over both the costs and quality
of its main suppliers disappeared with them. But for 40
years or more, GM's systems costing gave it an unbeatable advantage over even the most efficient of its competitors, which for most of that time was Studebaker.

Sears, Roebuck and Company was the first to copy
Durant's system. In the 1920s, it established long-term
contracts with its suppliers and bought minority inter-
ests in them. Sears was then able to consult with suppliers as they designed the product and to understand and
manage the entire cost stream. That gave the company
an unbeatable cost advantage for decades.

In the early 1930s, London-based department store
Marks & Spencer copied Sears with the same result.
Twenty years later, the Japanese, led by Toyota, studied
and copied both Sears and Marks & Spencer. Then in
the 1980s, Wal-Mart Stores adapted the approach by
allowing suppliers to stock products directly on store
shelves, thereby eliminating warehouse inventories and
with them nearly one-third of the cost of traditional
retailing.

But those companies are still rare exceptions. Although economists have known the importance of costing the entire economic chain since Alfred Marshall wrote about it in the late 1890s, most businesspeople still consider it theoretical abstraction. Increasingly, however, managing the economic cost chain will

When Sears switched to price-led costing, it was the exception. Now it's the rule.

become a necessity. In their article, "From Lean Production to the Lean Enterprise" (*Harvard Business Review,* March–April 1994), James P. Womack and Daniel T. Jones argue persuasively that executives need to organize and manage not only the cost chain but also everything else—especially corporate strategy and product planning—as one economic whole, regardless of the legal boundaries of individual companies.

A powerful force driving companies toward economic-chain costing will be the shift from cost-led pricing to price-led costing. Traditionally, Western companies have started with costs, put a desired profit margin on top, and arrived at a price. They practiced cost-led pricing. Sears and Marks & Spencer long ago switched to price-led costing, in which the price the customer is willing to pay determines allowable costs, beginning with the design stage. Until recently, those companies were the exceptions. Now price-led costing is becoming the rule. The Japanese first adopted it for their exports. Now Wal-Mart and all the discounters in the United States, Japan, and Europe are practicing price-led costing. It underlies Chrysler's success with its recent models and the success of GM's Saturn. Companies can practice price-led costing, however, only if they know and manage the *entire* cost of the economic chain.

The same ideas apply to outsourcing, alliances, and joint ventures—indeed, to any business structure that is built on partnership rather than control. And such entities, rather than the traditional model of a parent company with wholly owned subsidiaries, are increasingly becoming the models for growth, especially in the global economy.

Still, it will be painful for most businesses to switch to economic-chain costing. Doing so requires uniform or at least compatible accounting systems at companies along the entire chain. Yet each one does its accounting in its own way, and each is convinced that its system is the only possible one. Moreover, economic-chain costing requires information sharing across companies, and even within the same company, people tend to resist information sharing. Despite those challenges, companies can find ways to practice economic-chain costing now, as Procter & Gamble is demonstrating. Using the way Wal-Mart develops close relationships with suppliers as a model, P&G is initiating information sharing and economic-chain management with the 300 large retailers that distribute the bulk of its products worldwide.

Whatever the obstacles, economic-chain costing is going to be done. Otherwise, even the most efficient company will suffer from an increasing cost disadvantage.

Information for Wealth Creation

Enterprises are paid to create wealth, not control costs. But that obvious fact is not reflected in traditional measurements. First-year accounting students are taught that the balance sheet portrays the liquidation value of the enterprise and provides creditors with worst-case information. But enterprises are not normally run to be liquidated. They have to be managed as going concerns, that is, for *wealth creation*. To do that requires information that enables executives to make informed judgments. It requires four sets of diagnostic tools: foundation information, productivity information, competence information, and information about the allocation of scarce resources. Together, they constitute the executive's tool kit for managing the current business.

FOUNDATION INFORMATION

The oldest and most widely used set of diagnostic management tools are cash-flow and liquidity projections and such standard measurements as the ratio between dealers' inventories and sales of new cars; the earnings coverage for the interest payments on a bond issue; and the ratios between receivables outstanding more than six months, total receivables, and sales. Those may be likened to the measurements a doctor takes at a routine physical: weight, pulse, temperature, blood pressure, and urine analysis.

Until a business returns a profit that is greater than its cost of capital, it does not create wealth; it destroys it.

If those readings are normal, they do not tell us much. If they are abnormal, they indicate a problem that needs to be identified and treated. Those measurements might be called foundation information.

PRODUCTIVITY INFORMATION

The second set of tools for business diagnosis deals with the productivity of key resources. The oldest of them—

of World War II vintage—measures the productivity of manual labor. Now we are slowly developing measurements, though still quite primitive ones, for the productivity of knowledge-based and service work. However, measuring only the productivity of workers, whether blue or white collar, no longer gives us adequate information about productivity. We need data on *total-factor productivity*.

That explains the growing popularity of economic value-added analysis. EVA is based on something we have known for a long time: what we generally call profits, the money left to service equity, is usually not profit at all.[1] Until a business returns a profit that is greater than its cost of capital, it operates at a loss. Never mind that it pays taxes as if it had a genuine profit. The enterprise still returns less to the economy than it devours in resources. It does not cover its full costs unless the reported profit exceeds the cost of capital. Until then, it does not create wealth; it destroys it. By that measurement, incidentally, few U.S. businesses have been profitable since World War II.

By measuring the value added over *all* costs, including the cost of capital, EVA measures, in effect, the productivity of *all* factors of production. It does not, by itself, tell us why a certain product or a certain service does not add value or what to do about it. But it shows us what we need to find out and whether we need to take remedial action. EVA should also be used to find out what works. It does show which product, service, operation, or activity has unusually high productivity and adds unusually high value. Then we should ask ourselves, What can we learn from those successes?

The most recent of the tools used to obtain productivity information is benchmarking—comparing one's

performance with the best performance in the industry
or, better yet, with the best anywhere in business.
Benchmarking assumes correctly that what one organization does, any other organization can do as well. And
it assumes, also correctly, that being at least as good as
the leader is a prerequisite to being competitive.
Together, EVA and benchmarking provide the diagnostic tools to measure total-factor productivity and to
manage it.

COMPETENCE INFORMATION

A third set of tools deals with competencies. Ever since
C. K. Prahalad and Gary Hamel's pathbreaking article,
"The Core Competence of the Corporation" (*Harvard
Business Review*, May–June 1990), we have known that
leadership rests on being able to do something others
cannot do at all or find difficult to do even poorly. It
rests on core competencies that meld market or customer value with a special ability of the producer or
supplier.

Some examples: the ability of the Japanese to minia-
turize electronic components, which is based on their
300-year-old artistic tradition of putting landscape
paintings on a tiny lacquer box, called an *inro*, and of
carving a whole zoo of animals on the even tinier button
that holds the box on the wearer's belt, called a *netsuke;*
or the almost unique ability GM has had for 80 years to
make successful acquisitions; or Marks & Spencer's also
unique ability to design packaged and ready-to-eat luxury meals for middle-class budgets. But how does one
identify both the core competencies one has already and
those the business needs in order to take and maintain a
leadership position? How does one find out whether

one's core competence is improving or weakening? Or whether it is still the right core competence and what changes it might need?

So far the discussion of core competencies has been largely anecdotal. But a number of highly specialized midsize companies—a Swedish pharmaceutical producer and a U.S. producer of specialty tools, to name two—are developing the methodology to measure and manage core competencies. The first step is to keep careful track of one's own and one's competitors' performances, looking especially for unexpected successes and unexpected poor performance in areas where one should have done well. The successes demonstrate what the market values and will pay for. They indicate where the business enjoys a leadership advantage. The nonsuccesses should be viewed as the first indication either that the market is changing or that the company's competencies are weakening.

That analysis allows for the early recognition of opportunities. For example, by carefully tracking an unexpected success, a U.S. toolmaker found that small Japanese machine shops were buying its high-tech, high-priced tools, even though it had not designed the tools with them in mind or made

Every organization—not just businesses—needs one core competence: innovation.

sales calls to them. That allowed the company to recognize a new core competence: the Japanese were attracted to its products because they were easy to maintain and repair despite their technical complexity. When that insight was applied to designing products, the company gained leadership in the small-plant and machine-shop markets in the United States and Western Europe, huge markets where it had done practically no business before.

Core competencies are different for every organization; they are, so to speak, part of an organization's personality. But every organization—not just businesses—needs one core competence: *innovation.* And every organization needs a way to record and appraise its *innovative performance.* In organizations already doing that—among them several topflight pharmaceutical manufacturers—the starting point is not the company's own performance. It is a careful record of the innovations in the entire field during a given period. Which of them were truly successful? How many of them were ours? Is our performance commensurate with our objectives? With the direction of the market? With our market standing? With our research spending? Are our successful innovations in the areas of greatest growth and opportunity? How many of the truly important innovation opportunities did we miss? Why? Because we did not see them? Or because we saw them but dismissed them? Or because we botched them? And how well do we convert an innovation into a commercial product? A good deal of that, admittedly, is assessment rather than measurement. It raises rather than answers questions, but it raises the right questions.

RESOURCE-ALLOCATION INFORMATION

The last area in which diagnostic information is needed to manage the current business for wealth creation is the allocation of scarce resources: capital and performing people. Those two convert into action whatever information management has about its business. They determine whether the enterprise will do well or do poorly.

GM developed the first systematic capital-appropriations process about 70 years ago. Today practically every business has a capital-appropriations process, but few use it correctly. Companies typically measure their proposed capital appropriations by only one or two of the following yardsticks: return on investment, payback period, cash flow, or discounted present value. But we have known for a long time—since the early 1930s—that none of those is *the* right method. To understand a proposed investment, a company needs to look at *all* four. Sixty years ago, that would have required endless number crunching. Now a laptop computer can provide the information within a few minutes. We also have known for 60 years that managers should never look at just one proposed capital appropriation in isolation but should instead choose the projects that show the best ratio between opportunity and risks. That requires a capital-appropriations budget to display the choices—again, something far too many businesses do not do. Most serious, however, is that most capital-appropriations processes do not even ask for two vital pieces of information:

- What will happen if the proposed investment fails to produce the promised results, as do three out of every five? Would it seriously hurt the company, or would it be just a flea bite?

- If the investment is successful—and especially if it is more successful than we expect—what will it commit us to? No one at GM seems to have asked what Saturn's success would commit the company to. As a result, the company may end up killing its own success because of its inability to finance it.

In addition, a capital-appropriations request requires specific deadlines: When should we expect what results? Then the results—successes, near successes, near failures, and failures—need to be reported and analyzed. There is no better way to improve an organization's performance than to measure the results of capital appropriations against the promises and expectations that led to their authorization. How much better off the United States would be today had such feedback on government programs been standard practice for the past 50 years.

Capital, however, is only one key resource of the organization, and it is by no means the scarcest one. The scarcest resources in any organization are performing people. Since World War II, the U.S. military—and so far no one else—has learned to test its placement decisions. It now thinks through what it expects of senior officers before it puts them into key commands. It then appraises their performance against those expectations. And it constantly appraises its own process for selecting senior commanders against the successes and failures of its appointments. In business, by contrast, placement with specific expectations as to what the appointee should achieve and systematic appraisal of the outcome are virtually unknown. In the effort to create wealth, managers need to allocate human resources as purposefully and as thoughtfully as they do capital. And the outcomes of those decisions ought to be recorded and studied as carefully.

Where the Results Are

Those four kinds of information tell us only about the current business. They inform and direct *tactics*. For *strategy*, we need organized information about the environment. Strategy has to be based on information about markets, customers, and noncustomers; about technology in one's own industry and others; about worldwide finance; and about the changing world economy. For that is where the results are. Inside an organization, there are only cost centers. The only profit center is a customer whose check has not bounced.

Major changes also start outside an organization. A retailer may know a great deal about the people who shop at its stores. But no matter how successful it is, no retailer ever has more than a small fraction of the market as its customers; the great majority are noncustomers. It is always with noncustomers that basic changes begin and become significant.

At least half the important new technologies that have transformed an industry in the past 50 years came from outside the industry itself. Commercial paper, which has revolutionized finance in the United States, did not originate with the banks. Molecular biology and genetic engineering were not developed by the pharmaceutical industry.

Inside an organization, there are only cost centers. The only profit center is a customer whose check has not bounced.

Though the great majority of businesses will continue to operate only locally or regionally, they all face, at least potentially, global competition from places they have never even heard of before.

Not all of the needed information about the outside is available, to be sure. There is no information—not even unreliable information—on economic conditions in most of China, for instance, or on legal conditions in most of the successor states to the Soviet empire. But even where information is readily available, many businesses are oblivious to it. Many U.S. companies went into Europe in the 1960s without even asking about labor legislation. European companies have been just as blind and ill informed in their ventures into the United States. A major cause of the Japanese real estate investment debacle in California during the 1990s was the failure to find out elementary facts about zoning and taxes.

A serious cause of business failure is the common assumption that conditions—taxes, social legislation, market preferences, distribution channels, intellectual property rights, and many others—*must* be what we think they are or at least what we think they *should* be. An adequate information system has to include information that makes executives question that assumption. It must lead them to ask the right questions, not just feed them the information they expect. That presupposes first that executives know what information they need. It demands further that they obtain that information on a regular basis. It finally requires that they systematically integrate the information into their decision making.

A few multinationals—Unilever, Coca-Cola, Nestlé, the big Japanese trading companies, and a few big construction companies—have been working hard on building systems to gather and organize outside information. But in general, the majority of enterprises have yet to start the job.

Even big companies, in large part, will have to hire outsiders to help them. To think through what the business needs requires somebody who knows and understands the highly specialized information field. There is far too much information for any but specialists to find their way around. The sources are totally diverse. Companies can generate some of the information themselves, such as information about customers and noncustomers or about the technology in one's own field. But most of what enterprises need to know about the environment is obtainable only from outside sources—from all kinds of data banks and data services, from journals in many languages, from trade associations, from government publications, from World Bank reports and scientific papers, and from specialized studies.

Another reason there is need for outside help is that the information has to be organized so it questions and challenges a company's strategy. To supply data is not enough. The data have to be integrated with strategy, they have to test a company's assumptions, and they must challenge a company's current outlook. One way to do that may be a new kind of software, information tailored to a specific group—say, to hospitals or to casualty insurance companies. The Lexis database supplies such information to lawyers, but it only gives answers; it does not ask questions. What we need are services that make specific suggestions about how to use the information, ask specific questions regarding the users' business and practices, and perhaps provide interactive consultation. Or we might "outsource" the outside-information system. Maybe the most popular provider of the outside-information system, especially for smaller enterprises, will be that "inside outsider," the independent consultant.

Whichever way we satisfy it, the need for information on the environment where the major threats and opportunities are likely to arise will become increasingly urgent.

It may be argued that few of those information needs are new, and that is largely true. Conceptually, many of the new measurements have been discussed for many years and in many places. What is new is the technical data processing ability. It enables us to do quickly and cheaply what, only a few short years ago, would have been laborious and very expensive. Seventy years ago, the time-and-motion study made traditional cost accounting possible. Computers have now made activity-based cost accounting possible; without them, it would be practically impossible.

But that argument misses the point. What is important is not the tools. It is the concepts behind them. They convert what were always seen as discrete techniques to be used in isolation and for separate purposes into one integrated information system. That system then makes possible business diagnosis, business strategy, and business decisions. That is a new and radically different view of the meaning and purpose of information: as a measurement on which to base future action rather than as a postmortem and a record of what has already happened.

The command-and-control organization that first emerged in the 1870s might be compared to an organism held together by its shell. The corporation that is now emerging is being designed around a skeleton: *information*, both the corporation's new integrating system and its articulation.

Our traditional mind-set—even if we use sophisticated mathematical techniques and impenetrable sociological jargon—has always somehow perceived business as buying cheap and selling dear. The new approach defines a business as the organization that adds value and creates wealth.

Notes

1. I discussed EVA at considerable length in my 1964 book, *Managing for Results,* but the last generation of classical economists, Alfred Marshall in England and Eugen Böhm-Bawerk in Austria, were already discussing it in the late 1890s.

Originally published in January–February 1995
Reprint 95104

The Performance
Measurement Manifesto

ROBERT G. ECCLES

Executive Summary

THE LEADING INDICATORS OF BUSINESS PERFORMANCE cannot be found in financial data alone. Quality, customer satisfaction, innovation, market share—metrics like these often reflect a company's economic condition and growth prospects better than its reported earnings do. Depending on an accounting department to reveal a company's future will leave it hopelessly mired in the past.

More and more managers are changing their company's performance measurement systems to track nonfinancial measures and reinforce new competitive strategies. Five activities are essential: developing an information architecture; putting the technology in place to support this architecture; aligning bonuses and other incentives with the new system; drawing an outside resources; and designing an internal process to ensure the other four activities occur.

New technologies and more sophisticated databases have made the change to nonfinancial performance measurement systems possible and economically feasible. Industry and trade associations, consulting firms, and public accounting firms that already have well-developed methods for assessing market share and other performance metrics can add to the revolution's momentum—as well as profit from the business opportunities it presents.

Every company will have its own key measures and distinctive process for implementing the change. But making it happen will always require careful preparation, perseverance, and the conviction of the CEO that it must be carried through. When one leading company can demonstrate the long-term advantage of its superior performance on quality or innovation or any other nonfinancial measure, it will change the rules for all its rivals forever.

REVOLUTIONS BEGIN LONG BEFORE THEY ARE OFFICIALLY DECLARED. For several years, senior executives in a broad range of industries have been rethinking how to measure the performance of their businesses. They have recognized that new strategies and competitive realities demand new measurement systems. Now they are deeply engaged in defining and developing those systems for their companies.

At the heart of this revolution lies a radical decision: to shift from treating financial figures as the foundation for performance measurement to treating them as one among a broader set of measures. Put like this, it hardly sounds revolutionary. Many managers can honestly claim that they—and their companies—have tracked quality, market share, and other nonfinancial measures for years. Tracking these measures is one thing. But giving them equal (or even greater) status in determining strategy, promotions, bonuses, and other rewards is another. Until that happens, to quote Ray Stata, the CEO of Analog Devices, "When conflicts arise, financial considerations win out."[1]

The ranks of companies enlisting in this revolution are rising daily. Senior managers at one large, high-tech manufacturer recently took direct responsibility for adding customer satisfaction, quality, market share, and human resources to their formal measurement system. The impetus was their realization that the company's existing system, which was largely financial, undercut its strategy, which focused on customer service. At a smaller manufacturer, the catalyst was a leveraged recapitalization that gave the CEO the opportunity formally to reorder the company's priorities. On the new list, earnings per share dropped to last place, preceded by customer satisfaction, cash flow, manufacturing effectiveness, and innovation (in that order). On the old list, earnings per share stood first and almost alone.

In both companies, the CEOs believe they have initiated a sea change in how their managers think about business performance and in the decisions they make. Executives at other companies engaged in comparable efforts feel the same—rightly. What gets measured gets attention, particularly when rewards are tied to the measures. Grafting new measures onto an old accounting-driven performance system or making slight adjustments in existing incentives accomplishes little. Enhanced competitiveness depends on starting from scratch and asking: "Given our strategy, what are the most important measures of performance?" "How do these measures relate to one another?" "What measures truly predict long-term financial success in our businesses?"

DISSATISFACTION WITH USING FINANCIAL MEASURES to evaluate business performance is nothing new. As far back as 1951, Ralph Cordiner, the CEO of General Electric, commissioned a high-level task force to identify key corporate performance measures. (The categories the task force singled out were timeless and comprehensive: in addition to profitability, the list included market share, productivity, employee attitudes, public responsibility, and the balance between short- and long-term goals.) But the current wave of discontent is not just more of the same.

One important difference is the intensity and nature of the criticism directed at traditional accounting systems. During the past few years, academics and practitioners have begun to demonstrate that accrual-based performance measures are at best obsolete— and more often harmful.[2] Diversity in products, markets, and business units puts a big strain on rules and theories developed for smaller, less complex organizations. More dangerously, the numbers these systems generate often fail to support the investments in new technologies and markets that are essential for successful performance in global markets.

Managers' willingness to play the earning game calls into question the very measures the market focuses on.

Such criticisms reinforce concern about the pernicious effects of short-term thinking on the competitiveness of U.S. companies. Opinions on the causes of this mind-set differ. Some blame the investment community, which presses relentlessly for rising quarterly earnings. Others cite senior managers themselves, charging that their typically short tenure fosters shortsightedness. The important point is that the mind-set exists. Ask almost any senior manager and you will hear about some company's failure to make capital investments or pursue long-term strategic objectives that would imperil quarterly earnings targets.

Moreover, to the extent that managers do focus on reported quarterly earnings—and thereby reinforce the investment community's short-term perspective and expectations—they have a strong incentive to manipulate the figures they report. The extent and severity of such gaming is hard to document. But few in management deny that it goes on or that managers' willingness to play the earnings game calls into question the very measures the market focuses on to determine stock prices. For this reason, many managers, analysts, and financial economists have begun to focus on cash flow in the belief that it reflects a company's economic condition more accurately than its reported earnings do.[3]

Finally, many managers worry that income-based financial figures are better at measuring the consequences of yesterday's decisions than they are at indicating tomorrow's performance. Events of the past decade substantiate this concern. During the 1980s, many executives saw their companies' strong financial records deteriorate because of unnoticed declines in quality or customer satisfaction or because global competitors ate

into their market share. Even managers who have not
been hurt feel the need for preventive action. A senior
executive at one of the large money-center banks, for
example, grew increasingly uneasy about the European
part of his business, its strong financials notwithstand-
ing. To address that concern, he has nominated several
new measures (including customer satisfaction, customers' perceptions of the bank's stature and profes-
sionalism, and market share) to serve as leading indicators of the business's performance.

Discontent turns into rebellion when people
see an alternative worth fighting for. During the 1980s,
many managers found such an alternative in the quality
movement. Leading manufacturers and service
providers alike have come to see quality as a strategic
weapon in their competitive battles. As a result, they
have committed substantial resources to developing
measures such as defect rates, response time, delivery
commitments, and the like to evaluate the performance
of their products, services, and operations.

In addition to pressure from global competitors, a
major impetus for these efforts has been the growth of
the Total Quality Movement and related programs such
as the Malcolm Baldrige National Quality Award.
(Before a company can even apply for a Baldrige Award,
it must devise criteria to measure the performance of its
entire operation—not just its products—in minute
detail.) Another impetus, getting stronger by the day,
comes from large manufacturers who are more and
more likely to impose rigid quality requirements on their
suppliers. Whatever the stimulus, the result is the same:

quality measures represent the most positive step taken to date in broadening the basis of business performance measurement.

Another step in the same direction comes from embryonic efforts to generate measures of customer satisfaction. What quality was for the 1980s, customer satisfaction will be for the 1990s. Work on this class of measures is the highest priority at the two manufacturing companies discussed earlier. It is equally critical at another high-tech company that recently created a customer satisfaction department reporting directly to the CEO. In each case, management's interest in developing new performance measures was triggered by strategies emphasizing customer service.

As competition continues to stiffen, strategies that focus on quality will evolve naturally into strategies based on customer service. Indeed, this is already happening at many leading companies. Attention to customer satisfaction, which measures the quality of customer service, is a logical next step in the development of quality measures. Companies will continue to measure quality on the basis of internally generated indexes (such as defect rates) that are presumed to relate to customer satisfaction. But they will also begin to evaluate their performance by collecting data directly from customers for more direct measures like customer retention rates, market share, and perceived value of goods and services.

Just as quality-related metrics have made the performance measurement revolution more real, so has the development of competitive benchmarking.[4] First, benchmarking gives managers a methodology that can be applied to any measure, financial or non-financial, but that emphasizes nonfinancial metrics. Second (and less obvious), it has a transforming effect on managerial mind-sets and perspectives.

Benchmarking involves identifying competitors and/or companies in other industries that exemplify best practice in some activity, function, or process and then comparing one's own performance to theirs. This externally oriented approach makes people aware of improvements that are orders of magnitude beyond what they would have thought possible. In contrast, internal yardsticks that measure current performance in relation to prior period results, current budget, or the results of other units within the company rarely have such an eye-opening effect. Moreover, these internally focused comparisons have the disadvantage of breeding complacency through a false sense of security and of stirring up more energy for intramural rivalry than for competition in the marketplace.

Finally, information technology has played a critical role in making a performance measurement revolution possible. Thanks to dramatically improved price-performance ratios in hardware and to breakthroughs in software and database technology, organizations can generate, disseminate, analyze, and store more information from more sources, for more people, more quickly and cheaply than was conceivable even a few years back. The potential of new technologies, such as hand-held computers for employees in the field and executive information systems for senior managers, is only beginning to be explored. Overall, the range of measurement options that are economically feasible has radically increased.

Veterans know it is easier to preach revolution than to practice it. Even the most favorable climate can create only the potential for revolutionary change. Making it happen requires conviction, careful preparation, per-severance, and a decided taste for ambiguity. As yet, there are no clear-cut answers or predetermined processes for managers who wish to change their measurement systems. Based on the experience of companies engaged in this revolution, I can identify five areas of activity that sooner or later need to be addressed: developing an information architecture; putting the technology in place to support this architecture; aligning incentives with the new system; drawing on outside resources; and designing a process to ensure that the other four activities occur.

Developing a new information architecture must be the first activity on any revolutionary agenda. *Information architecture* is an umbrella term for the categories of information needed to manage a company's busi-nesses, the methods the company uses to generate this information, and the rules regulating its flow. In most companies, the accounting system implicitly defines the information architecture. Other performance measures are likely to be informal—records that operating man-agers keep for themselves, for instance—and they are rarely integrated into the corporate-driven financial system.

The design for a new corporate information architec-ture begins with the data that management needs to pursue the company's strategy. This may sound like a truism, but a surprising number of companies describe their strategies in terms of customer service, innovation, or the quality and capabilities of their people, yet do lit-tle to measure these variables. Even time—the newest strategic variable—remains largely underdeveloped in terms of which time-based metrics are most important and how best to measure them.

As part of this identification process, management
needs to articulate a new corporate grammar and define
its own special vocabulary—the basic terms that will
need to be common and relatively invariant across all
the company's businesses. Some of these terms (like
sales and costs) will be familiar. Others, however, will
reflect new strategic priorities and ways to think about
measuring performance. For example, both a large
money-center bank and a multidivisional, high-technology manufacturer introduced the use of cross-company
customer identification numbers so they could readily
track such simple and useful information as the total
amount of business the company did with any one customer. It sounds elementary and it is—as soon as you
start to look at the entire measurement system from
scratch.

Uniformity can be carried too far. Different businesses with different strategies require different information for decision making and performance measurement. But this should
not obscure the equally
obvious fact that every
company needs to have
at least a few critical
terms in common.

*One high-tech company has
reorganized 24 times in the
past 4 years to keep pace
with changes in its markets.*

Today few large companies do. Years of acquisitions and
divestitures, technological limitations, and at times, a
lack of management discipline have all left most big
organizations with a complicated hodgepodge of definitions and variables—and with the bottom line their only
common denominator.

Developing a coherent, company wide grammar is
particularly important in light of an ever-more stringent
competitive environment. For many companies, ongoing

structural reorganizations are a fact of life. The high-technology company described above has reorganized itself 24 times in the past 4 years (in addition to a number of divisional and functional restructurings) to keep pace with changes in its markets and technologies. Rather than bewail the situation, managers relish it and see their capacity for fast adaptation as an important competitive advantage.

A common grammar also enhances management's ability to break apart and recombine product lines and market segments to form new business units. At a major merchant bank, for example, the organization is so fluid that one senior executive likens it to a collection of hunting packs that form to pursue business opportunities and then disband as the market windows on those opportunities close. The faster the company can assemble information for newly formed groups, the greater the odds of success. So this executive (who calls himself the czar of information) has been made responsible for developing standard definitions for key information categories.

How a company generates the performance data it needs is the second piece of its information architecture. Not surprisingly, methods for measuring financial performance are the most sophisticated and the most deeply entrenched. Accountants have been refining these methods ever since double-entry book-keeping was invented in the fifteenth century. Today their codifications are enforced by a vast institutional infrastructure made up of professional educators, public accounting firms, and regulatory bodies.

In contrast, efforts to measure market share, quality, innovation, human resources, and customer satisfaction have been much more modest. Data for tracking these measures are generated less often: quarterly, annual, or even biannual bases are common. Responsibility for them typically rests with a specific function. (Strategic planning measures market share, for example, while engineering measures innovation and so on.) They rarely become part of the periodic reports general managers receive.

Placing these new measures on an equal footing with financial data takes significant resources. One approach is to assign a senior executive to each of the measures and hold him or her responsible for developing its methodologies. Typically, these executives come from the function that is most experienced in dealing with the particular measure. But they work with a multifunctional task force to ensure that managers throughout the company will understand the resulting measures and find them useful. Another, less common, approach is to create a new function focused on one measure and then to expand its mandate over time. A unit responsible for customer satisfaction might subsequently take on market share, for example, or the company's performance in human resources.

Unlike a company's grammar, which should be fairly stable, methods for taking new performance measures should evolve as the company's expertise increases. Historical comparability may suffer in the process, but this is a minor loss. What matters is how a company is doing compared with its current competitors, not with its own past.

The last component of a corporate information architecture is the set of rules that governs the flow of information. Who is responsible for how measures are taken? Who actually generates the data? Who receives and analyzes them? Who is responsible for changing the rules? Because information is an important source of power, the way a company answers these questions matters deeply. How open or closed a company is affects how individuals and groups work together, as well as the relative influence people and parts of the company have on its strategic direction and management. Some companies make information available on a very limited basis. At others, any individual can request information from another unit as long as he or she can show why it is needed. Similarly, in some companies the CEO still determines who gets what information—not a very practical alternative in today's world. More often what happens is that those who possess information decide with whom they will share it.

Advances in information technology such as powerful workstations, open architectures, and relational databases vastly increase the options for how information can flow. It may be centralized at the top, so that senior executives can make even more decisions than they have in the past. Or it may be distributed to increase the decision-making responsibilities of people at every level. The advantages of making information widely available are obvious, though this also raises important questions that need to be addressed about the data's integrity and security. In principle, however, this portion of the information architecture ought to be the most flexible of the three, so that the company's information flows continue to change as the conditions it faces do.

DETERMINING THE HARDWARE, SOFTWARE, AND TELECOMMUNICATIONS TECHNOLOGY a company needs to generate its new measurement information is the second activity in the performance revolution. This task is hard enough in its own right, given the many choices available. But too often managers make it even harder by going directly to a technology architecture without stopping first to think through their information needs. This was the case at a high-tech manufacturing company that was growing more and more frustrated with its information systems planning committee. Then the CEO realized that he and the other senior managers had not determined the measures they wanted before setting up the committee. Equipped with that information, the committee found it relatively easy to choose the right technology.

Once the information architecture and supporting technology are in place, the next step is to align the new system with the company's incentives—to reward people in proportion to their performance on the measures that management has said truly matter. This is easier said than done. In many companies, the compensation system limits the amount and range of the salary increases, bonuses, and stock options that management can award.

In companies that practice pay-for-performance, compensation and other rewards are often tied fairly mechanically to a few key financial measures such as profitability and return on investment. Convincing managers that a newly implemented system is really going to be followed can be a hard

Formulas that tie incentives to performance look objective—and rarely work.

sell. The president of one service company let each of his division general managers design the performance measures that were most appropriate for his or her particular business. Even so, the managers still felt the bottom line was all that would matter when it came to promotions and pay.

The difficulty of aligning incentives to performance is heightened by the fact that formulas for tying the two together are rarely effective. Formulas have the advantage of looking objective, and they spare managers the unpleasantness of having to conduct truly frank performance appraisals. But if the formula is simple and focuses on a few key variables, it inevitably leaves some important measures out. Conversely, if the formula is complex and factors in all the variables that require attention, people are likely to find it confusing and may start to play games with the numbers. Moreover, the relative importance of the variables is certain to change more often—and faster—than the whole incentive system can change.

For these reasons, I favor linking incentives strongly to performance but leaving managers free to determine their subordinates' rewards on the basis of all the relevant information, qualitative as well as quantitative. Then it is up to the manager to explain candidly to subordinates why they received what they did. For most managers, this will also entail learning to conduct effective performance appraisals, an indirect—and invaluable—benefit of overhauling the measurement system.

Outside parties such as industry and trade associations, third-party data vendors, information technology companies, consulting firms, and public accounting firms must also become part of the performance measurement revolution. Their incentive: important business opportunities.

Industry and trade associations can play a very helpful role in identifying key performance measures, researching methodologies for taking these measures, and supplying comparative statistics to their members— so can third-party data vendors. Competitors are more likely to supply information to a neutral party (which can disguise it and make it available to all its members or customers) than to one another. And customers are more likely to provide information to a single data vendor than to each of their suppliers separately.

Consulting firms and information technology vendors also have important roles to play in forwarding the revolution. Firms that specialize in strategy formulation, for example, often have well-developed methods for assessing market share and other performance metrics that clients could be trained

Public accounting firms have what may be the single most critical role in this revolution.

to use. Similarly, firms that focus on strategy implementation have a wealth of experience designing systems of various kinds for particular functions such as manufacturing and human resources. While many of these firms are likely to remain specialized, and thus require coordination by their clients, others will surely expand their capabilities to address all the pieces of the revolution within a client company.

Much the same thing is apt to happen among vendors of information technology. In addition to helping companies develop the technological architecture they need, some companies will see opportunities to move into a full range of services that use the hardware as a technology platform. IBM and DEC are already moving in this direction, impelled in part by the fact that dramatic gains in price-performance ratios make it harder and harder to make money selling "boxes."

Finally, public accounting firms have what may be the single most critical role in this revolution. On one hand, they could inhibit its progress in the belief that their vested interest in the existing system is too great to risk. On the other hand, all the large firms have substantial consulting practices, and the revolution represents a tremendous business opportunity for them. Companies will need a great deal of help developing new measures, validating them, and certifying them for external use.

Accounting firms also have an opportunity to develop measurement methods that will be common to an industry or across industries. While this should not be overdone, one reason financial measures carry such weight is that they are assumed to be a uniform metric, comparable across divisions and companies, and thus a valid basis for resource allocation decisions. In practice, of course, these measures are not comparable (despite the millions of hours invested in efforts to make them so) because companies use different accounting conventions. Given that fact, it is easy to see why developing additional measures that senior managers—and the investment community—can use will be a massive undertaking.

Indeed, the power of research analysts and investors generally is one of the reasons accounting firms have such a crucial role to play. Although evidence exists that investors are showing more interest in metrics such as market share and cash flow, many managers and analysts identify the investment community as the chief impediment to revolution.[5] Until investors treat other measures as seriously as financial data, they argue, limits will always exist on how seriously those measures are taken inside companies.

GE's experience with its measurement task force supports their argument. According to a knowledgeable senior executive, the 1951 effort had only a modest effect because the measures believed to determine the company's stock price, to which incentives were tied, were all financial: earnings per share, return on equity, return on investment, return on sales, and earnings growth rate. He believed that once the financial markets valued other measures, progress within companies would accelerate.

Would managers be willing to publish anything more than the financial information the SEC requires?

Investors, of course, see the problem from a different perspective. They question whether managers would be willing to publish anything more than the financial information required by the SEC lest they reveal too much to their competitors. Ultimately, a regulatory body like the SEC could untie this Gordian knot by recommending (and eventually requiring) public companies to provide nonfinancial measures in their reports. (This is, after all, how financial standards became so omnipotent and why so many millions of hours have been invested in their development.) But I suspect competitive pressure will prove a more immediate force for change. As soon as one leading company can demonstrate the long-term advantage of its superior performance on quality or innovation or any other non-financial measure, it will change the rules for all its rivals forever. And with so many serious competitors tracking—and enhancing—these measures, that is only a matter of time.

D ESIGNING A PROCESS to ensure that all these things happen is the last aspect of the revolution. To overcome conservative forces outside the company and from within (including line and staff managers at every level, in every function), someone has to take the lead. Ultimately, this means the CEO. If the CEO is not committed, the revolution will flounder, no matter how much enthusiasm exists throughout the organization.

But the CEO cannot make it happen. Developing an information architecture and its accompanying technology, aligning incentives, working with outside parties— all this requires many people and a lot of work, much of it far less interesting than plotting strategy. Moreover, the design of the process must take account of the integrative nature of the task: people in different businesses and functions including strategic planning, engineering, manufacturing, marketing and sales, human resources, and finance will all have something to contribute. The work of external players will have to be integrated with the company's own efforts.

Organizationally, two critical choices exist. One is who the point person will be. Assigning this role to the CEO or president ensures its proper symbolic visibility. Delegating it to a high-level line or staff executive and making it a big piece of his or her assignment may be a more effective way to guarantee that enough senior management time will be devoted to the project.

The other choice is which function or group will do most of the work and coordinate the company's efforts. The CEO of one high-tech company gave this responsibility to the finance function because he felt they should have the opportunity to broaden their perspective and measurement skills. He also thought it would be easier to use an existing group experienced in performance measurement. The president of an apparel company made a different choice. To avoid the financial bias embedded in the company's existing management information systems, he wanted someone to start from scratch and design a system with customer service at its core. As a result, he is planning to combine the information systems department with customer service to create a new function to be headed by a new person, recruited from the outside.

What is most effective for a given company will depend on its history, culture, and management style. But every company should make the effort to attack the problem with new principles. Some past practices may still be useful, but everything should be strenuously challenged. Otherwise, the effort will yield incremental changes at best.

Open-mindedness about the structures and processes that will be most effective, now and in the future, is equally important. I know of a few companies that are experimenting with combining the information systems and human resource departments. These experiments have entailed a certain amount of culture shock for professionals from both functions, but such radical rethinking is what revolution is all about.

Finally, recognize that once begun, this is a revolution that never ends. We are not simply talking about changing the basis of performance measurement from financial statistics to something else. We are talking about a new philosophy of performance measurement that regards it as an ongoing, evolving process. And just as igniting the revolution will take special effort, so will maintaining its momentum—and reaping the rewards in the years ahead.

Combining information systems and human resources is a culture shock for both departments. But that's what revolution is all about.

Notes

1. Ray Stata, "Organizational Learning—The Key to Management Innovation," *Sloan Management Review*, Spring 1989, pp. 63–74.

2. Donald A. Curtis, "The Modern Accounting System," *Financial Executive*, January–February 1985, pp. 81–93; and H. Thomas Johnson and Robert S. Kaplan, *Relevance Lost* (Boston: Harvard Business School Press, 1987).

3. Yuji Ijiri, "Cash Flow Accounting and Its Structure," *Journal of Accounting, Auditing, and Finance*, Summer 1978, pp. 331–348.

4. Robert C. Camp, *Benchmarking* (Milwaukee, Wisconsin: ASQS Quality Press, 1989).

5. "Investors: Look at Firms' Market Share," *Wall Street Journal*, February 26, 1990, pp. C1–2.

Originally published in January–February 1991
Reprint 91103

Tapping the Full Potential
of ABC

JOSEPH A. NESS AND THOMAS G. CUCUZZA

Executive Summary

MANY COMPANIES HAVE USED ACTIVITY-BASED COST-
ING in onetime profitability studies. But when companies
integrate ABC into critical management systems and use
it to make day-to-day decisions—when they use it as
activity-based management—it becomes a powerful tool
for continuously rethinking and improving a business.

Most managers do not realize that implementing
activity-based management is a major organizational-
change effort that involves a tremendous amount of
work. The biggest obstacle is resistance from employees. The authors focus on two companies—Chrysler Corporation and Safety-Kleen Corporation—whose success
in implementing activity-based management can serve
as a model for other companies. The benefits they have
reaped have been 10 to 20 times their investments in
their programs.

Both companies persuaded critical employees, such as plant managers, to give activity-based management a try, then used their success to persuade others. They tackled ongoing business problems to show, rather than tell, employees how activity-based management could expand the business and, as a result, jobs. Both began with one plant, then methodically rolled the system out into the entire organization, involving local managers at each stage. Both invested in educating employees at all levels in the principles and mechanics of activity-based management. And once it had been introduced at a work site, both quickly dumped the old accounting system.

M ANY COMPANIES HAVE USED ACTIVITY-BASED COSTING (ABC) in onetime profitability studies to help them decide which products or customers to cut or keep. But ABC can be much more than a superior accounting technique that shows how much money individual products are really making or losing. When ABC is woven into critical management systems, it can serve as a powerful tool for continuously rethinking and dramatically improving not only products and services but also processes and market strategies.

To use ABC in that fashion involves managing in a radically different way. And that, of course, means the people in a business—from the CEO to frontline workers—must change radically, too. No wonder so many companies have found *activity-based management* so much more difficult to implement than they had imagined.

Thousands of companies have adopted or explored the feasibility of adopting ABC. However, we estimate that no more than 10% of them now use activity-based management in a significant number of their operations. The other 90% have given up, or their programs are stagnating or floundering.

The problem is that managers often do not think of activity-based management as a major organizational-change program. It is. Combing the organization to pinpoint all the useful information about the direct and indirect costs of a product or service is a huge undertaking. So is setting up an information system that can track those cost-contributing activities and present them in formats that employees can use.

Educating employees at all levels about the principles and the mechanics of ABC may be the most difficult task of all. Employees must understand thoroughly what the company is trying to achieve through ABC as well as how to use it in their jobs. They must be convinced that ABC can succeed and that it is worth the effort. To win over employees, each company needs a carefully crafted rollout that takes into account its culture and operating idiosyncrasies.

Finally, other management systems need to be overhauled to ensure that employees fully incorporate ABC into their work practices and do not retreat to their old practices in times of stress and self-doubt. The old accounting system has to be rooted out as quickly as possible. Measurement and incentive systems have to be tied to the ABC numbers. And the daily decision-making process—including

Employee resistance is the single biggest obstacle to implementing ABC.

which managers are involved in making decisions and how they make them—often must be significantly altered, too. A major reason so few efforts have succeeded is that managers fail to take all those steps. Admittedly, they are difficult steps to take.

Like any major organizational-change program, ABC invariably runs up against employee resistance. Indeed, in the companies we have worked with, employee resistance has been the single biggest obstacle. Such resistance is natural. Managers of a unit—whether a function, a division, or a plant—are understandably nervous about revealing detailed information that could be used to attack their practices or undermine their authority. It would be naïve expect managers to rejoice at being asked to replace a cost-accounting system they are used to with one that could dramatically change the definitions of success and failure. And after having been downsized, TQMed, and reengineered, managers and nonmanagers alike, not surprisingly, often greet ABC as the latest threat to their jobs.

Nonetheless, the effort required to weave activity-based thinking into the fabric of a company's way of managing is worth it. When managers adopt activity-based management, they use ABC to find answers to questions such as the following: What should a given product or process cost? What are the non-value-adding activities that contribute to its current cost? If a given distribution channel or market is unprofitable, where can the company reduce costs to make it profitable? If the company eliminates an unprofitable product or customer, how much will it save in

Activity-based management helps companies become the one everyone else is copying.

costs? If the company lowers the price of a product to increase sales volume, what will the impact on the cost per unit be? And what can the company do during the design and engineering stages of a product to avoid unnecessary costs in the first place?

For many managers, the standard approach for improving a business is to benchmark each function or process against the company they think is the best in that function or process. But activity-based management enables companies to leapfrog the best—to become the company everyone else is copying. Activity-based management makes possible dramatic, rather than incremental, improvements. Consider the benefits reaped by two companies: Chrysler Corporation, a company whose ABC implementation effort we have studied, and Safety-Kleen Corporation, a client that we helped with installing ABC.

Chrysler estimates that, since it began implementing ABC in 1991, the system has generated hundreds of millions of dollars in benefits by helping simplify product designs and eliminate unproductive, inefficient, or redundant activities. The benefits have been 10 to 20 times greater than the company's investment in the program. At some sites, the savings have been 50 to 100 times the implementation cost.

Since Safety-Kleen, a midsize waste-recycling company, introduced ABC into its organization, also in 1991, it has reaped more than $12.7 million in cost savings, cost avoidance, and increased revenues—more than 14 times its investment in the program. The company, based in Elgin, Illinois, has used ABC to prune product lines, rationalize operations, and expand into new markets. Even more important, ABC has helped Safety-Kleen transform itself from an organization whose individual operations made decisions based on what each one—rightly or wrongly—thought best for itself into an organization whose operations now make day-in, day-out decisions that are best for the whole company.

To illustrate the obstacles that managers are likely to encounter when they try to install ABC and the ways in which they might overcome those hurdles, we will look at Chrysler and Safety-Kleen in detail. The outstanding success of their ABC programs is not the only reason we chose them as models.

Another is that they have more operations using ABC and have integrated ABC into critical management systems to a greater degree than most other companies. More than two-thirds of Chrysler's manufacturing and assembly plants in the United States, all of its Mopar replacement-parts operations, its finance arm, and the company's well-known cross-functional platform teams now use ABC. And plans call for the whole company to use performance measures based on ABC-generated numbers by the year 2000. At Safety-Kleen, the corporate laboratory and 7 of its 11 recycling operations have integrated ABC totally into their financial and performance-measurement systems.

A third reason we focused on Chrysler and Safety-Kleen is to illustrate the range of approaches a company can take. At Chrysler, Robert A. Lutz, the company's president and chief operating officer, decided that he wanted the organization to use ABC and then made sure it did every step of the way. At Safety-Kleen, a middle manager initiated a pilot project at one plant and then used its success to win over executives and other plants' managers.

Although the two companies arrived at the decision to adopt ABC by different paths, both believed that a new approach to cost management was necessary to achieve their long-term strategies. Both understood that, instead of an accounting system designed to control expenditures, they needed a system that would help managers make better decisions about which products or services to offer and how to make and sell them. Both ran into many of the obstacles that other companies have encountered. Unlike many companies, Chrysler and Safety-Kleen recognized that they were not merely changing their accounting systems; they were changing their organizations. That understanding heavily influenced the way they rolled out ABC, and it is why their stories offer valuable lessons for other companies interested in activity-based management.

Turning to ABC

Chrysler, which has $52 billion in revenues and 123,000 employees, 97,000 of those in the United States, turned to ABC to help transform a bureaucratic organization set in its ways. During the 1980s, the automotive giant made enormous strides in improving its operating efficiency, slashing costs, boosting quality, and rejuvenating its product line. Nonetheless, Chrysler ended the decade still playing catch-up to such formidable competitors as the Japanese automakers and Ford Motor Company. Chrysler's financial crisis in the late 1980s, its second in a decade, underscored how much work remained to be done.

Chrysler's leaders were determined to replace the company's hierarchical functional structure with one that was much more flexible, efficient, cross-functional, and process oriented. To that end, they pushed the company to create its platform teams for developing new vehicles and to forge closer links with suppliers and distributors. Encouraged by the teams' initial successes in the late 1980s, they decided to transform the entire company into a process-focused organization.

Lutz, who had championed the platform teams and was the driving force behind the decision to structure the whole company around processes, became the leading advocate for using ABC to help with the transformation. He knew how difficult getting employees to change would be, especially with the auto market beginning to rebound and the company's profits rising. He believed that ABC would buttress the process approach by showing how much each process actually cost and by exposing inefficiencies.

Few at Chrysler believed the old accounting system gave an accurate picture of the company's costs.

The main purpose of the old cost-accounting system had been to help the finance department monitor operations and value inventory. However, outside of finance, few people believed the old system provided an accurate picture of the company's costs. One of the skeptics was Lutz. During his career at Ford, BMW, and Chrysler, he had often been annoyed when his creative proposals for product designs and manufacturing-process improvements were rejected. Because the companies' financial systems focused on direct costs and relied on arbitrary cost allocations, such as labor-based overhead rates, he felt they were incapable of evaluating his proposals fairly. His frustrations resurfaced during the rollout of the platform teams at Chrysler. Once again, Lutz saw clearly that the company's cost-accounting system could not report costs by process, much less separate value-added from non-value-added activities. When he came across an article about activity-based costing, he said, "This is the system for me."

In contrast, Safety-Kleen, a relatively young, fast-growing company, turned to ABC because it had out-grown its accounting system. Safety-Kleen was founded in 1968 in response to companies' crying need to find safe ways to remove and recycle their hazardous wastes. The company started out processing one type of waste—mineral spirits—in one plant in Illinois and needed only a basic cost-accounting system that could provide suffi-cient information to satisfy internal financial controls and investors. The company's main challenge was how to exploit the vast opportunities in an undeveloped mar-ket. It was a marketing-driven company focused on envi-ronmental compliance; efficiency of operations was a secondary concern.

By 1991, however, Safety-Kleen had become much bigger and much more complex. The number of haz-ardous chemicals it handled had grown to more than 100, and the number of product lines had grown to ten, including used motor oil, antifreeze, oil filters, paint, and dry-cleaning solvents. And its number of plants had grown to 12 in eight states and Puerto Rico, and most of them handled multiple types of waste. (One plant has since been closed.) By the early 1990s, the market had also become more complex. Growth had slowed, compe-tition had increased, and some states had begun impos-ing taxes of up to 25% on hazardous-waste generators and recyclers.

Safety-Kleen, which currently has 6,600 employees and revenues of $800 million, achieved its rapid growth by encouraging the managers of its facilities to act like entrepreneurs. Plant managers were responsible for deciding how to handle the wastes shipped to their facilities; they could process the material themselves or ship it to another facility or, in some cases, to a third-party processor. But usually, wastes were simply shipped to the nearest Safety-Kleen plant, whether or not it was the one that could process them at the lowest cost. In fact, Safety-Kleen did not know the true costs of its services and products. The main purpose of the cost-accounting numbers was to help the accounting department keep the books, not to help operations do its job.

As the pressure on profits intensified, so did operations' and marketing's animosity toward accounting because they didn't trust its numbers. Operations and marketing began to develop their own numbers to support decisions about capital expenditures, pricing, plant utilization, and process improvements. Top management gradually realized that the company needed to start basing waste-handling decisions on what would generate the most profits for the whole company rather than what would be best for an individual plant. In order to make decisions that way, the company needed much more detailed information about its operational costs, including how much processing, shipping, and handling a given batch of materials would cost at each plant. In short, the company needed a radically new cost-accounting system.

Internal Resistance

When Safety-Kleen and Chrysler first introduced ABC, they both quickly discovered that many employees—from frontline workers to senior managers to entire departments—resisted. Some feared ABC would change the existing power structure. Some felt threatened

because they knew ABC would reveal inefficient practices that had been hidden by the traditional cost-
accounting systems. Others did not like ABC, simply
because it was new. And many managers, especially
those who felt ABC was being imposed on their operations, resisted because they knew installing it was a
tremendous amount of work. (See "Why Collecting ABC
Information Is Such a Big Job, " on page 70.)

The deep skepticism with which Chrysler employees
greeted the ABC initiative at some of the first work sites
where it was installed was hardly surprising. Chrysler
had a long history of flavor-of-the-month performance-
improvement programs that never seemed to deliver
what they promised and were replaced as soon as a new
program came along. The fact that one division had
briefly tried a form of ABC in the mid-1980s and had
abandoned it after a change in management only fed the
skepticism.

As Lutz had anticipated, once the market had
rebounded, employees questioned why the company
needed to change at all. Furthermore, with all plants
operating at full tilt, line and middle managers questioned whether they had the time to collect the necessary data. Many employees also feared that an unspoken
motive for introducing ABC was to eliminate jobs. Some
of the corporate controller's staff and some operations
managers were equally unenthusiastic. The old cost-
accounting system had shaped their skills and their way
of thinking about costs. They, too, assumed that ABC
was just the latest fad and that once it had passed, life
would continue relatively unchanged.

The initial resistance at Safety-Kleen was different,
partly because a middle manager in accounting was the
effort's champion. The notion that ABC might greatly

help Safety-Kleen originated with C. James Schulz, the
controller of North American operations, who recruited

*When the accountants
arrived at Safety-Kleen's
plant in New Castle,
Kentucky, the manager told
them to get lost.*

William J. Chaika, the
assistant controller of
the recycling centers, to
undertake a pilot
project. Schulz and
Chaika's bosses—the
corporate controller and

the chief financial officer—approved and supported the
project, but Chaika was the one who actively championed the effort.

Senior managers had chosen a plant in New Castle,
Kentucky, as the pilot because they wanted to use it to
enter a new growth market. Before plunging ahead, they
wanted to make sure they knew the actual costs of processing materials with new multimillion-dollar equipment at the plant. Chaika assembled a team of three
Safety-Kleen regional controllers, one financial analyst,
and two consultants from Price Waterhouse to join him
in installing an ABC system. When they arrived at the
plant, the trouble began. The manager told them to get
lost. As far as he was concerned, accounting had no
business telling him how to run his plant.

Chaika also ran into resistance from the vice president of recycle-center operations, to whom all the plant
managers reported, and the five marketing vice presidents, who were each responsible for one or more lines
of hazardous waste. Operations and marketing agreed
that the company needed to change the way it made
decisions, but they had different priorities. Marketing
wanted information on product costs, and operations
wanted information on operating performance. Neither
department was happy that the initiative had come out

of accounting. In addition, each feared the other would use the numbers to invade its turf. And the five marketing vice presidents were fearful that ABC would change the ground rules for calculating profits and, as a result, might reduce their pay.

After some initial struggles, both Chrysler and Safety-Kleen overcame internal resistance in ways that serve as a model for other companies. First, both companies persuaded critical employees to give ABC a fair shake and, ultimately, to embrace the system. Second, both mounted major programs to educate employees at all levels in the principles and mechanics of ABC. Third, both began with one plant and then rolled out the program throughout their organizations, making sure that local managers were involved and that there were visible successes. Finally, once ABC had been introduced at a facility, they quickly dumped the old accounting system.

Getting Widespread Acceptance

At many companies, top management delegates the implementation of ABC to the accountants. We think that practice is a mistake. At Chrysler, executives got involved from the start, a commitment that continues today. For example, Chrysler's operating committee of senior executives, which Lutz chairs, has taken responsibility for tracking and guiding the ABC program on a regular basis. In addition, Chrysler's officers—its top 32 executives—spend half a day once a year in a workshop in which they receive in-depth briefings on the rollout's progress and deliberate about where the company should install ABC next.

Lutz also decided that finance alone should not control the emerging ABC system. Instead, he gave joint responsibility for the system to James D. Donlon III, the controller, and James P. Holden, the vice president who is in charge of continuous improvement and the move to process management. The project team that has spearheaded the implementation program reports to both executives. In addition, both Lutz and Robert J. Eaton, Chrysler chairman and CEO, became vocal advocates of ABC throughout the company. At work site after work site, both have preached that a process-based structure using ABC could make Chrysler the most agile, lowest-cost automaker in North America by 1996 and in the world by 2000.

Safety-Kleen used a different approach to gain employee acceptance. First, Chaika pacified the manager of the New Castle plant by promising that if he didn't agree that ABC helped him make better decisions by the end of the pilot project, he could abandon it. Within three months, everyone could see that ABC would help the plant cut costs significantly. (In the first year, ABC helped the plant identify a hefty $3.5 million in potential annual cost savings.) Equally important, the ABC numbers were extremely helpful in figuring out the amount of new materials that the plant needed to process in order to be competitive and profitable. The plant's manager was sold.

Chaika then orchestrated special meetings with operations and marketing and with senior executives, a group that included the vice president of recycle-center operations and the five marketing vice presidents. Chaika and his team went over the plant's 150-page cost book in great detail, showing how costs had been allocated to different

After seeing what ABC could do, plant managers clamored to get on board.

processes and how the cost of each product had been derived. No one could argue with the numbers. Everyone realized that such numbers would help them make better decisions, which would quickly generate higher profits.

Chaika did not have to woo the managers of the other plants. After seeing the difference ABC was making at New Castle, they clamored to get on board.

Training the Workforce

No company that we know of has invested the time and effort that Chrysler has in educating employees about ABC. More than 18,000 Chrysler employees have attended one of the company's formal ABC training courses. Many union officials and suppliers' employees have taken the courses, too. From the outset, the courses have had two main purposes: to explain why ABC is necessary and to instruct employees in how to set it up and use it. Chrysler created three groups of courses.

The courses in the first group, which introduce the basic concepts of ABC, are for employees at a wide range of levels—from top management down to some hourly workers. The half-day courses explain what ABC is, how it differs from the traditional cost-accounting system, and what Chrysler hopes to get out of it. The message, reinforced with examples, is that ABC's purpose is to help employees make better decisions, not to get them to work harder or to eliminate their jobs.

The courses in the second group are for managers who will have responsibility for implementing ABC at their work sites. The two-day courses make heavy use of case studies and cover the practical application of ABC information in making decisions. For example, a computerized simulation lets people tackle realistic business problems, such as whether the company should start manufacturing a part that it now buys from a supplier. The computer program first uses traditional financial information, which allocates many costs arbitrarily, and then ABC information. Most participants figure out the best solution when they use the ABC numbers. In contrast, the answers—and the outcomes—vary widely when they use the numbers from the old accounting system. "Those with good intuition do well, while those without good intuition go bankrupt," says David E. Meador, the Chrysler manager who heads the company's ABC implementation team.

The courses in the third group, which last three to five days, are highly technical and specialized. Their purpose is to teach employees such as industrial engineers, controllers, and investment analysts how to set up and use an ABC-based system—in other words, the skills needed to collect the data, build the models, set up the computer systems, and analyze the information.

Safety-Kleen never offered formal classroom training in ABC. Instead, it put employees through a three-month, intensive, on-the-job training program—an approach that makes sense for many smaller companies. After the first-day fiasco at New Castle, Chaika realized that he could not impose ABC on a plant. Every aspect—from collecting the data, to designing the system, to training the workforce to interpret and use the data—had to be done in partnership with the plant's management. So, at New Castle and later at other plants, the implementation team first spent two days explaining to the plant's managers all the steps involved in installing ABC, emphasizing that the process would be a joint effort. The team also stressed that the main reason for installing ABC was to help managers expand the business, not shrink it, and it pointed to how ABC had led to hiring, not firing, at the first plants.

After the data had been collected and the system had been designed at a particular plant, the team and the plant's managers made a top-ten list of ways they thought that efficiency could be improved. The team then helped the plant's personnel analyze the projects, in the process teaching them how to use ABC and showing how it could help them make better decisions. For example, the Safety-Kleen plant in Linden, New Jersey, analyzed the company's practice of temporarily storing used motor oil at hazardous-waste-processing centers before shipping it to its oil-recycling plant in East Chicago, Indiana. When Safety-Kleen entered the market for recycling motor oil, it used available tank capacity at hazardous-waste centers in order to reduce transportation costs. Using small trucks, the centers collected the oil from service stations within a 150-mile radius. Once a center had enough to fill a big tanker truck, it loaded the oil again and transported it 10 to 25 miles to a rail yard, where it was shipped to East Chicago. Because Safety-Kleen had tank capacity available at its centers, managers considered it a free resource. But an ABC-based analysis showed that the *cost* of using it certainly was not free. First, the company had not calculated the costs of testing each batch of oil in the truck, unloading it, testing it again in the tank, reloading it into a larger truck, and retesting it in that truck. Second, the company had not considered the cost of unnecessary paperwork: Although oil is not a hazardous

At every plant, the team stayed until the staff had put at least two or three improvements in place.

material, the company had to document its handling as if it were in order to comply with regulations for hazardous-waste centers. Once the company tallied all of those costs and charged them to the oil-recycling business, the practice quickly stopped. The small trucks began taking the oil directly to the rail yard.

At every plant where ABC was implemented, the team stayed until the staff was able to put at least two or three items on its top-ten list into action. It made sure that the benefits were quantified—both to drive home to the plant's employees the difference that ABC had made and to win over people at other plants. In instance after instance, plant managers said that ABC helped them make decisions that they previously had had a gut feeling were right but had been reluctant to make without hard data. ABC, they said, gave them the data they needed.

The Rollout

Chrysler's managers, like Safety-Kleen's, realized fairly quickly that they had to take great care to make sure that employees felt involved in ABC's introduction and saw proof that it really worked. Chrysler's first step was to expose top-level managers to the concept in a series of seminars. Then, in 1991, Chrysler launched a pilot project at its high-volume stamping plant in Warren, Michigan. Chrysler's managers chose Warren because it looked like a sure win. The plant had a progressive manager, and company executives believed that its product mix could be improved. Over time, the plant had been pressed into making some low-volume parts, and executives had strong hunches that their true costs were much higher than the traditional cost-accounting system indicated.

The pilot was extremely successful. The ABC numbers showed that the actual costs of some low-volume parts were as much as 30 times the stated costs, which made clear that the company would be much better off outsourcing those parts and making more high-volume parts. In addition, the pilot helped uncover pockets of waste and inefficiency, which plant managers attacked immediately. Finally, it helped the plant redesign both its products and processes so that it could make parts for the company's next minivan model much more efficiently.

Two-thirds of the way into the rollout at Warren, the results were already so impressive that Lutz decided to introduce ABC at six more plants. He assigned Donlon, the controller, the job of getting the effort under way. Donlon handpicked 6 young, aggressive employees to be on the initial ABC implementation team. All came from the finance department. But as the rollout began to pick up steam over the next year, the team's full-time staff was increased to 20. To reinforce the message that the motive for installing ABC was to help the managers run their operations better, the team's membership also was broadened to include people from manufacturing, engineering, and information systems. The team's composition certainly helped the ABC program achieve the high level of acceptance that it has won throughout the company.

Chrysler methodically rolled out ABC into all areas of the company to show it was for everyone, not just manufacturing.

Chrysler refined the introduction process into a science and methodically rolled out ABC into all areas of the company in order to emphasize that it was for everyone, not just manufacturing. The entire rollout at a work site takes 6 to 15 months, depending on the size of the facility. First, an advance group conducts 12 weeks of training to pave the way for the actual installation of ABC. During that period, everyone at the work site takes one or more of the courses the company offers, and managers widely distribute videos and newsletter articles on what is to come. They also encourage the people who will be responsible for setting up and using the ABC system to attend sessions aimed at making them receptive to new ideas. Next, two other groups arrive on the scene to implement the ABC system and to give the operation's managers and professionals hands-on training in using its information and maintaining and updating the system. The first group oversees the efforts to collect data and build the ABC computer model. The second helps with the technical work required to link the ABC model with the general ledger, the manufacturing-planning system, and other support systems. Both groups work closely with the managers of the operation—to tap their knowledge and to instill in them a sense of ownership of both the rollout and the new ABC system.

Chrysler's managers also realized that they had to show, rather than merely tell, employees that ABC would help them make better decisions. For example, ABC helped Chrysler tackle a long-standing problem: how to determine the optimal number of wiring harnesses—the wiring packages used for a vehicle's electrical systems—that it should design and produce for a new minivan. The alternatives ranged from one to nine.

If the company produced only one, that harness would have to contain wires for all the possible options. On the other hand, if the company produced nine harnesses, each one tailored to a particular type of van, it would waste less material but would incur greater costs and make the design and production processes more complex. Because design engineers were measured by how well they kept down the materials costs for each vehicle, they voted for nine. Because manufacturing plant managers were rewarded for minimizing inventory and labor, they wanted to produce only one. But the ABC team showed that making two harnesses would strike the best balance between minimizing waste and maximizing productivity. Once they saw the ABC numbers, neither the design engineers nor the manufacturing managers could dispute that conclusion.

After Safety-Kleen had installed the ABC pilot at its New Castle plant, operations and marketing executives took a strategic approach to selecting the next plants. The goal was to use the rollout to get an overview of the relative costs and profitability of each recycling process and line of business. If the decision between two plants utilizing the same process was a toss-up, they chose the plant whose manager seemed more enthusiastic.

Safety-Kleen tried to strike a balance between maximizing the speed of the rollout and minimizing the number of people on the implementation teams. To that end, the company limited the number of work sites at which ABC was being introduced at any one time to two and staggered the two efforts. A core team of three people—the regional controller, an accounting analyst, and, until the company felt it had mastered the process, a Price Waterhouse consultant—oversaw each introduction from the beginning to the end. Five others—analysts who assisted with process mapping, data collection, and activity costing—performed their tasks and then left. A typical implementation took three months at the plant and a week to tie in the plant's new ABC system to corporate headquarters.

Because of the plant-by-plant approach, the corporate accounting department was not able to convert to ABC all at once. Only after all the targeted plants had been converted could the controller's staff streamline and automate its own closing process. The result: Even though ABC requires more data collection, reporting, and analysis than the traditional accounting system did, closing the books each month now takes no longer than before.

Within 15 months of the pilot's launch, operations, marketing, and accounting executives had begun to use ABC information to make strategic decisions. And within 18 months of the launch, Safety-Kleen's five largest plants had adopted it.

Final Integration

The final hurdle in implementing ABC is integrating it into the organization's financial systems and performance measures. Many companies have tried to implement ABC as a shadow or secondary system. But ABC won't take root if its numbers are not integrated into the company's mainstream financial-reporting system. When the ABC data are not kept up to date, can't be reconciled with the financial reports, or are not distributed widely as the official numbers, managers often retreat to the old numbers. "If two sets of numbers exist, one set will ultimately dominate," says Donlon, the controller at Chrysler, which tried using ABC as a shadow system at some of its first sites.

Most companies develop stand-alone ABC models, which they install on off-line personal computers. Those models often can't be integrated into the official financial results, are difficult to maintain, and usually do not follow generally accepted accounting principles, which means they cannot be used for external financial reporting. As a result, they quickly become obsolete.

Precisely because maintaining one set of numbers is difficult enough, let alone two, Safety-Kleen's management decided that as soon as an ABC system had been introduced into a work site, it should become the sole source of financial-reporting numbers. In the recycling centers, the company installed a new data-collection system that could update the ABC numbers each month. It also built automatic links between its corporate general ledger and the ABC system to ensure that the numbers reconciled in both systems every month.

Safety-Kleen now uses ABC numbers to develop its annual budget and to make strategic decisions about closing plants and adding and cutting product lines. Safety-Kleen also has adopted ABC-based performance measures, which involved a fundamental rethinking of the old system. As Safety-Kleen rolled out ABC, its top-level managers realized that some of the old performance measures were not motivating plant managers to make decisions that were best for the company as a whole. For example, plant managers were still rewarded based on how they performed against an operating budget set at the beginning of each year, which did not take into account processing efficiency or unit costs. The measures were changed to reward managers for reducing the unit costs of the materials processed at their plants.

When used in a onetime analysis of products' costs, ABC can make a big difference. But it is a onetime big difference. After a company has integrated ABC into all of its mainstream financial systems, and ABC numbers have become the yardsticks of performance, the system dramatically changes the way an organization's people think. Then, the average quality of the decisions made day in and day out will be vastly higher than before. When that happens, you can bet that the company's performance will show it.

Why Collecting ABC Information Is Such a Big Job

MOST COMPANIES SERIOUSLY UNDER-ESTIMATE how big a job gathering the information needed to set up an ABC system is. One reason is that ABC is much more detailed and complex than standard cost accounting. Traditional systems lump together many costs into a few heterogeneous overhead pools, or categories. Under ABC, each of those pools are often broken into scores of ABC activities, and it may take hundreds of inquiries to identify and gather the information on them. Similarly, an ABC system uses many more statistical measures to assign the overhead costs to products, processes, distribution channels, customers, and markets than a traditional system does. A standard system typically uses one or two statistical measures, such as the number of hours of direct labor required to make each product, to allocate overhead costs to products. A typical ABC system uses dozens of cost drivers, ranging from the number of parts to the number of sales calls, to allocate activity costs.

Another reason collecting data is so time-consuming, especially in the beginning, is that figuring out precisely what kind of information is required to set up an ABC system and where to find it takes a while. Most companies go overboard at first and end up with a mountain of excruciatingly detailed information, which overwhelms both their people and their computer systems. When Chrysler installed ABC at its first factory, a stamping plant in Warren, Michigan, it gathered three times the information it could use practically. Because of that overkill, collecting the information took twice the resources that it would now, given Chrysler's knowledge and experience. Similarly, Chrysler's Mopar replacement-parts operation found itself overwhelmed by data when it attempted to construct ABC costs for each of the 250,000 parts that it stocks. Mopar ultimately decided to construct the costs of 60 major and minor product groups, which reduced the amount of data to a manageable level but was still extremely useful.

Safety-Kleen also found that less could be more. When its ABC implementation team was helping plants set up ABC systems, many of the plants' managers pressed the team to include an extraordinary amount of detail in the ABC models. The team, however, grew worried that the detail would overwhelm the ABC systems and concluded that much of the requested information was not important for determining costs. When the managers persisted, the ABC team got them to accept a compromise: 75% of the information would be included in the ABC model, and the team would set up another statistical performance-reporting system to track the rest.

Originally published in July–August 1995
Reprint 95408

How High Is Your Return on Management?

ROBERT SIMONS AND ANTONIO DÁVILA

Executive Summary

THE CLASSIC BUSINESS RATIOS FOR MEASURING PER-
FORMANCE—return on equity, return on assets, and return
on sales, to name a few—may be useful. But none is
designed specifically to reflect how well a company
implements its strategy. Enter return on management
(ROM), a new ratio that gauges the payback from a
company's scarcest resource: managers' time and
energy. Unlike other business ratios, ROM is a rough estimate, not an exact percentage. Still, it is expressed like
other business ratios by an equation in which the output is
maximized by a high numerator and a low denominator:

$$\frac{\text{Productive organizational energy released}}{\text{Management time and attention invested}}$$

Knowing which organizational factors conspire
against or work to maximize an organization's produc-

tive energy will help managers calculate a rough measure for this equation.

The authors suggest that companies look at five factors—referred to as the "five acid tests"—to approximate this measure: Do employees know which opportunities do not directly contribute to the company's strategic mission? Do managers know what it would take for the company to fail? Can managers recall their key diagnostic measures with relative ease? Is the organization free from drowning in a sea of paperwork and processes? Do all employees watch the same performance measures that their bosses watch? If a manager can answer yes to these question, ROM is probably high. If the answer is no to some, ROM may be low, signaling that managers may need to step up their communication with employees about what they should and should not be focusing their efforts on.

VIRTUALLY EVERY MANAGER HAS A STORY about a brilliant strategy that got away. Everyone supported the strategy, so the story goes, but somehow it was never implemented. Or maybe the strategy *was* implemented—but only haphazardly. These stories always seem to end in the same way: frustration, lost opportunity, occasionally crisis—and often utter confusion. Why is it, many managers wonder, that such a large percentage of the most reasonable, analysis-driven, *implementable* strategies never make it from concept to reality?

The answer lies with managers themselves—or more specifically, with how managers direct their energy. Managerial energy is an organization's most important and most scarce resource, especially in these days of boundless opportunity. New opportunities seem to pop up monthly—what with falling trade barriers, emerging markets, and technological breakthroughs—all tugging on a manager's time and attention and filling up his or her date book.

But if managerial energy is misdirected or diffused over too many opportunities, even the best strategies stand little chance of being implemented and translated into value. That simple fact drives the most formidable and important task in business today: making sure managers are channeling their energies into the right projects or issues. Yes, this sounds logical enough in theory, but in the hypercharged, high-intensity environment of today's corporate fray, perhaps nothing is harder than keeping oneself—and one's organization—on strategy's straight and narrow.

What to do? We recommend that managers use a new business ratio. We call it *return on management* (ROM), and it can be expressed as the following equation:

$$\text{ROM} = \frac{\text{Productive organizational energy released}}{\text{Management time and attention invested}}$$

Like its cousins, return on equity and return on assets, ROM measures the payback from the investment of a scarce resource—in this case, a manager's time and attention. It indicates how well managers have chosen among alternative courses of action to deploy that resource optimally. The ratio answers the question, Are you getting the maximum payback from every hour of the day that you invest in implementing your business's strategy?

But first things first: ROM is not a quantitative formula: it does not generate a specific number or percentage. Instead, it is a qualitative measure: both the numerator and denominator, and the equation's result are estimates of magnitude that managers must construe in their minds and guts. ROM's output is directional; like all quantitative return ratios, ROM is maximized when the numerator is large and the denominator is

ROM measures the payback from the investment of a company's scarcest resource—managers' time and attention.

small. By using the ratio, managers can "calculate" if their ROM is high, medium, or low. It's a rough measure, but we have found that executives who understand ROM's value possess a powerful tool for understanding and for change.

For an example of how ROM works, consider two companies. The first is a small Boston-based consulting company—let's call it Automation Consulting Services—that started out with a clear strategy of specializing in industrial technology.[1] The company grew quickly off the base of its expertise and soon expanded to four offices. But seven years after its founding, the company was in a severe crisis. In one of the offices, staff were discovered to be cross-charging clients to meet budget requirements. In another office, management had failed to detect a drop in the amount of business generated by three of the company's largest auto-manufacturing clients, which was leaving much of the professional staff idle. In a third office, an excursion into the uncharted waters of automating a client company's library had resulted in financial losses and embarrassment as the consulting company realized that it did not possess the skills to deliver on the contract.

Simply put, the company had come undone. Managers were spreading their energy over too many projects, clients, and goals with no sense of priorities. At one time, the company had possessed a sound and focused strategy: growth through providing clients with state-of-the-art industrial technology. But managers had allowed the many opportunities facing the business to disperse their efforts away from implementing that strategy. As a result, the amount of productive organizational energy released was extremely low, but the amount of management time invested was very high. The company's ROM was dismal.

By contrast, Automatic Data Processing (ADP)—a large database-processing company, headquartered in Roseland, New Jersey—provides a clear example of a company in which managers understand the value of focusing their energy around the projects that directly serve the company's strategy. By using a strict checklist to assess whether projects are consistent with the company's strategy and by clearly communicating a list of the company's priorities, ADP has achieved 143 consecutive quarters (make that 35 years) of double-digit, earnings-per-share growth—a record unmatched by any other company traded on the New York Stock Exchange. Not surprisingly, ADP's ROM is sky high.

What separates these two organizations is plain: at ADP, managerial energy is riveted on specific, crystal-clear strategic priorities only for the amount of time it takes to get results. Certainly, the managers at both companies are aware that the world is teeming with business opportunities, but at ADP, managers also know there are only so many hours in a day and only so many managers to go around. Like all high-ROM managers, they have realized that organizations thrive when their leaders—and those who work for them—are disciplined in how they spend their time. Instead of trying to capture every flag like Automation Consulting Services tried to do, they make hard choices about where they will commit their energy and, more important, where they won't. This clarity of purpose transforms all energy into productive energy and propels strategy from the boardroom to the marketplace.

The Enemies and Allies of High ROM

If, as we've suggested, focusing managerial energy pays such high dividends, why don't all managers intuitively work to maximize ROM? The first answer is that many natural organizational forces conspire against the discipline of ROM. We've already mentioned the plethora of marketplace opportunities that beckon managers today. Second, people naturally fight the fire that is closest to their feet, just as managers naturally attend to the most pressing crisis, apparently promising project, or demanding client. Third, even well-intentioned processes, such as performance review programs, that should focus a company on strategy implementation have a way of growing bureaucratic and ponderous in organizational settings. And finally, the reason why many managers don't use ROM as a guide is that, frankly, it's difficult. It requires constant vigilance. Managing day to day is hard enough without steadfastly looking out for the symptoms of organizational confusion or strategic drift.

And so, the behaviors that contribute to low ROM invariably creep in—that is to say, unless managers first recognize them and then prevent or reverse them. The following five questions are designed primarily to help managers determine whether the enemies of high ROM have infiltrated their organizations. But these "acid tests" also suggest how managers can put ROM-inspired management into action. They are as much about empowering the allies of high ROM as they are about rooting out its enemies. (See "Return on Management [ROM]: An Overview," on page 95.)

You may already have a rough sense of your organization's ROM, but for a more precise reading, try answering the following questions:

Acid Test #1: Does your organization know what opportunities are out of bounds? In most companies, strategy formulation begins in the stratosphere. That is to say, strategy begins with a broad and grandly stated mission statement, usually along the following lines: "Our mission is to apply the talents, knowledge, and skills of our employees to make ABC Corporation the leader in all of the markets we serve. We will exert great effort to deliver innovative products at a fair price, ensuring that we are the preferred provider for our customers."

This kind of motivational message is an important first step, but it then must be brought down to earth. Senior managers have this job. They translate the mission statement into short- and long-term strategic plans, budgets, and so forth. But often something goes awry in this process. The organization, inspired by the mission statement and the ambitious strategic plans that fall out of it, are left with an overly vague sense of how to spend their energy.

To combat this phenomenon, high-ROM managers take a different but complementary approach. Not only do they tell their employees about their vision for the company, but they also spell out what opportunities are off limits—in other words, they identify how their employees *cannot* spend their time. High-ROM managers are explicit, for example, in telling their employees what types of customers the organization *will not* accept, what types of products or initiatives it *will not* fund, what types of deals people *should not* do. They establish strategic boundaries that move beyond the platitudes of a mission statement to the hard choices at the core of successful strategy implementation.

At ADP, for example, managers use a checklist that identifies which business opportunities are verboten. It covers every strategic base:

Financial. No opportunities that cannot generate $50 million in annual revenue.

Growth. No opportunities that cannot generate at least 15% continuing growth rate.

Competitive Position. No opportunities where ADP cannot be first or second in the market.

Products. No new products that cannot be sold on the mass market, that cannot be mass produced, or that do not offer consistently superior direct-client service and performance features.

Sustained Market Position. No opportunities that do not put products or services in a very distinctive position, that do not include plans for adding a significant number of new clients, and that do not offer a high payback for clients.

With such an explicit guide, it is not surprising that ADP has never veered off its strategic course.[2]

Microsoft CEO Bill Gates is similarly unequivocal about setting strategic boundaries: "To be very clear, we are not going to own any telecommunications networks: phone companies, things like that. We're not going to do system integration or consulting for corporate information systems. We love to write software, but there are exceptions. You won't see us doing applications like small-business accounting. That's a nice area for some people, but not for us. Computer-aided design and engineering? We won't be doing that."

By contrast, senior managers at Automation Consulting Services never framed or communicated their strategy in terms of the opportunities that were out of bounds. As a result, lower-level managers chased every mildly promising contingency. The result? They spent untold hours on the library automation project—a project related to a market in

ROM has a way of plunging—and fast—when managers let themselves or their employees engage in activities that fall outside of the company's strategic boundaries.

which the organization did not have a competitive advantage and was not planning to develop any. Managers were so distracted they failed to notice that three major clients in their core market were slowly slipping away. Nor did they notice the serious ethical problem of double billing clients.

In our experience, most managers understand the need to impose codes of business conduct on employees in order to stem potential losses of assets or of the company's reputation. Too few managers, however, understand the importance of setting strategic boundaries to protect employees from wasting the company's most valuable asset—the energy and focus needed to implement a strategy.

Strategic boundaries, it should be noted, are useless unless policed. That's also part of the work of high-ROM

managers. Naturally, some opportunities that fall outside a company's strategy can look attractive. They can
look, in fact, like low-hanging fruit—easy for the picking.
A high-ROM manager must say no in these instances. A
case in point is one private retail bank that wanted to
refocus its strategy on affluent customers who could
generate at least $5,000 in annual net revenue. In sup-
port of that strategy, the company told its bank managers and employees *not* to bring in new business that
did not meet this criterion. Employees pushed back.
"What happens if someone walks in off the street and
wants to do a lucrative onetime foreign-exchange trans-
action?" they asked. "Should we send them down the
street to a competitor?" Managers responded with an
unequivocal "Yes!" Above all, they wanted to avoid the
myriad day-to-day distractions that slowly sap organizational energy away from implementing the strategic
agenda.

To conclude, then, high ROM is very much about setting limits. High-ROM managers view every choice
about their activities through the prism of strategy
implementation. They
ask, "Will this meeting
help move our strategic
agenda forward?" and
"Does this client's prob-
lem deserve the energy
and time we are devoting
to it given the company's strategy?" With clear strategic
boundaries, managers can avoid the insidious trap of
allowing everyone to put a small amount of resources
behind all manner of good ideas that are not tightly
aligned with the strategy of the business. By deciding to
pass up certain opportunities, managers can ensure that

*High-ROM managers have
a healthy fear of what it
would take for their
company to unravel, or
worse—fail outright.*

everyone in the organization is working toward the same explicit goals. All energy becomes productive.

Acid Test #2: Are your company's critical performance measures driven by a healthy fear of failure? The fact that strategy often eludes implementation is not surprising to most managers. That's why so many companies are now linking strategy to performance measures. For instance, companies that base their strategy on customer service evaluate their employees on their ability to anticipate and respond to the needs of customers.

Generally speaking, linking strategy to performance measures is a robust idea—the kind that supports high ROM. But the real challenge for managers is making sure employees are evaluated for the performance factors that really matter to strategy. Too often, managers succumb to a form of political correctness in determining performance factors. In order not to offend any division or constituency within the company, they compile long lists of critical performance variables—such as information-processing

In low-ROM companies, no one is certain which performance variables are being measured and why.

productivity, employee satisfaction, and revenue growth—but do not differentiate what is supposedly nice to have from what is truly critical to the company's success. As a result, people don't know exactly where they should focus their time. Energy disperses, and ROM suffers.

Consider the case of a financial services company where managers hired consultants to help them design performance scorecards. They identified more than a dozen critical performance variables and included reciprocal feedback loops that traced the variables' value to the business. Included were product innovation, employee training, customer satisfaction, employee commitment, organizational renewal, and many other "key" drivers of business success. Each item was duly substantiated by deductive analysis of cause and effect. The resulting diagrams with their myriad loops, arrows, and ovals were truly impressive to behold. Unfortunately, the scorecards were so all encompassing that they did not provide guidance about priorities. In fact, employees leaving the meeting were unable to articulate which of the performance variables were mission-critical to the strategy of the business.

High-ROM managers use the fancy charts and graphs as a foundation for the more important work ahead— deciding what *will not* be on the list of critical performance measures. To do so, they need to visualize their worst fears. They should close their eyes and imagine the unimaginable: five years hence, their strategy has failed. They should ask themselves what went wrong. What didn't they do right? What competitor or market trend did they miss? How did they fail to execute their strategy? All the consultants' and staff reports in the world are no substitute for this often gut-wrenching exercise. It may not be elegant, but it tells managers exactly which performance variables make the difference between success and failure. These are the critical performance variables—the only ones with which high-ROM managers should be concerned.

What can happen if a company does not follow this path? Consider the case of a start-up that invented a new medical-imaging device. Once the new device had proved its economic potential, a major pharmaceutical company acquired the company. The final price of the purchase, however, was contingent on the start-up's sales and profit growth during the next five years. The founding management team, which had a significant equity stake in the company, elected to stay on to run the business.

The earn-out payments, which kicked in during the third year, were the result of achieving aggressive sales and profit goals. That was not surprising since throughout the five-year period, senior managers had instructed everyone in the organization to focus his or her attention on maximizing these two financial measures. They had even promised a cash bonus and a one-week trip to Hawaii to every employee if the company met its financial goals.

The goals were met. But employees had cut corners in the process, prompting a warning letter from the FDA that threatened the company with closure if it did not improve the quality of its product. In response, management linked year-end bonuses to quality (in addition to profitability). And indeed, during the final two years of the earn-out, the company achieved the required quality standards and avoided FDA action. It did not, however, fully meet its financial goals.

The year after the earn-out was complete, sales at the company declined 40%. The reason was painfully simple: a competitor had introduced a new and better technology. Ironically, the company's managers—in their fixation on short-term goals—had not envisioned strategic failure or focused their employees' energy on preventing it. If they had, employees would have been evaluated first and foremost on their ability to generate technological innovations.

High-ROM managers have the courage to imagine what it would take for their company to crash and burn. This assessment then becomes the backbone of their performance-measurement system. A high level of information technology productivity or employee retention may be wonderful to have, but it may contribute little to long-term success. Not every performance variable matters. Managers who use ROM as their guide are willing—even eager—to be "politically incorrect" in the name of organizational focus and strategy implementation.

Acid Test #3: Can managers recall their key diagnostic measures? Another syndrome afflicting many low-ROM companies is fixating on too many diagnostic measures. In other words, companies use too many figures to hold their managers and employees accountable for performance—measures such as ROCE, sales growth, renewal rates, and cash flow. As we've said, performance should be measured along only those dimensions that truly matter to success. Similarly, people should be held accountable only for as many diagnostic measures as they can memorize. We would suggest that the limit be seven.

Why seven? If people are given too few challenges, there won't be enough variety in their work to stimulate creativity. If people are given too many challenges, they quickly suffer from overload. Seven falls between these two extremes. And think of all the things in our lives that are configured in sevens: phone numbers, the days of the week, the musical scale. The number seems to contain just the right amount of information for people to remember and process effectively.[3] Successful management frameworks—such as the 7-S analysis, the Seven Steps of Quality, and the Seven Habits of Highly Effective People—have leveraged this universal fact.

This is not to say that everyone in an organization should be held accountable for exactly seven measures or that everyone should be held accountable for the same ones. Different divisions, even different employees, must pay attention to different indicators of a business's health. Moreover, different diagnostic measures should be selected and assigned depending on the organization's place in its life cycle.

Take the example of one electronics company, where senior management used between four and seven diagnostic measures at any given time to communicate strategy effectively to the organization. At the company's inception, cash flow was critical to survival, and senior management galvanized the company around measures intended to shorten the cash cycle. When cash flow came under control, the ability to meet product performance standards consistently became critical, and management focused its attention on indicators of product quality. In recent years, as the organization has matured, managers have redefined their diagnostic measures to focus on product development, manufacturing quality, and customer service. But importantly, they have been particularly careful not to confuse the organization by holding people accountable for more measures than they can store in their memories.

As the president of the electronics company says, "I can guide the organization through our changing marketplace by holding people accountable for just a small number of measures. Everyone can tell you what those measures are and why they're important to our success. Of course, I have to be able to change the measures when necessary. But it's critical to keep the number of measures down so that there is no ambiguity about where people should be focusing their energy."

Acid Test #4: Is your organization safe from drowning in a sea of paperwork and processes? When the new CEO of a high-technology company with sales more than $3 billion first took on his position, he summarily killed the company's strategy-management process. The process had previously spanned a nine-month period from early December to early September. During that time, managers at all levels reviewed their strategy and created their plans and budgets. The result of this energy-intensive process was a "book" for each division that was several inches thick. It included an in-depth analysis of the company's industry, customers, environment, and competitive position; detailed one-year and five-year operating and investment plans for each of the functions in the division; risk assessments of the proposed strategies; and a detailed budget for the coming year as well as projected three-year trends.

Among the worst enemies of ROM are paperwork and processes that weigh managers down and prevent them from spending time and energy on competitive challenges that matter.

Such analysis sounds useful in theory, but the process itself absorbed an enormous amount of energy from top-level managers throughout the company. Meetings, negotiations, presentations, and back-and-forth exchanges of thousands of pages of memos were diverting managers' attention away from profitable activities. Form was driving out substance. The new CEO saw the investment of managerial talent in the strategic planning process as a low-ROM investment.

This is just one example of how well-meaning management processes can go awry—or even backfire.

Remember management-by-objectives, zero-based budgeting, strategic planning, and total quality management? What became of these much-heralded breakthroughs in management techniques? In each case, managers ultimately rebelled because of demands imposed on their time—demands that had little to do with creating value for shareholders, customers, or employees.

Take the case of total quality management at Florida Power & Light. This company was an exemplar of TQM methods, winning the Deming Award and later starting a TQM consulting practice. Interestingly, however, a new CEO shut down the company's TQM program because he felt that the system—which demanded frequent management meetings and an untold number of reports—had pulled managers away from the company's real work to the point that customers and the bottom line were suffering for it.

At high-ROM companies, planning, budgeting, and control systems operate differently: they are exception based—alerting managers to anomalies to sound practice. Think of the thermostat in your home. Once you set the desired temperature to 68° F, how much of your personal attention is required to keep the air temperature at the desired level? The answer, of course, is none. The system lifts the burden of monitoring from your shoulders, freeing you to do other, more important things. Those of you who are engineers will recognize the thermostat as a negative feedback system. It continuously monitors actual temperature, compares it with desired temperature, and activates remedial action when shortfalls are sensed.

That is how the majority of control systems and related processes work in high-ROM companies. Managers can ignore them most of the time. They set annual goals, receive periodic exception reports, and get on with the business of strategy implementation. Process has a way of drowning an organization. If you feel as though your organization is submerged in paperwork and meetings, there is a good chance that the enemies of high ROM are part of the undertow.

Acid Test #5: Does everyone watch what the boss watches? There is a well-known—and very instructive— story about Robert Galvin when he was CEO of Motorola. (Galvin ran Motorola from 1964 to 1986.)

If your organization is submerged in paperwork and meetings, there's a good chance the enemies of high ROM are part of the undertow.

Galvin was so fixated on making Motorola the world leader in quality, it is said, that he walked out of meetings when quality was not the topic. Similarly, he would leave divisional performance reviews after the quality figures were discussed—he would simply stand up and leave the room after hearing a quantitative report on the quality of the products made by various divisions. It was clear to everyone: the boss's goal was product perfection.

The same kind of unmistakable message about priorities was sent to managers at Pepsi-Cola when Don Kendall was CEO. As John Sculley, who was president of Pepsi at the time, recalled, "The Nielsens defined the ground rules of competition for everyone at Pepsi-Cola. They were at the epicenter of all we did. They were the nonpublic body counts of the Cola Wars. Pepsi-Cola's top managers would carry little charts in their wallets with the latest key Nielsen figures. They became such an important part of my life that I could quote them on any product in any market. We would pore over the data using it to search for Coke's vulnerable points where an assault could successfully be launched or to explore why Pepsi had slipped a fraction of a percentage point in the game." Sculley added, "The company wasn't always this way. The man at the front of the table made it so."[4]

In high-ROM organizations, everyone knows what the boss watches—and they watch the same thing themselves. The challenge for bosses, therefore, is to make sure that everyone in the organization is aware of what they should be watching—whether it's quality ratings or Nielsen rankings. By getting everyone in the organization focused on the same thing, high-ROM managers are able to direct all the company's energy toward the same cause.

What does the boss watch? At high-ROM companies, everyone is watching it too.

How do high-ROM managers signal what matters to them? Typically, by their actions rather than their words. Although high-ROM managers let most control processes run on automatic pilot, they invariably pick one or two control systems to fixate on. They use the measures generated by these systems to engage the organization in heated discussion and debate.

These *interactive* control systems are unique because, instead of monitoring business as usual, they focus organizational energy on the uncertain-ties inherent in executing the company's strategy successfully. At Pepsi-Cola, managers used the Nielsen data to test their assumptions about the effects of pricing, promotion, and packaging on market demand and competitors' actions. Within an hour of receiving such data, 60 or 70 people at Pepsi would examine the information generated by the selected control system. In face-to-face meetings, they would then ask questions such as, What assumptions could upset our plans? What are our competitors doing? and Is new technology affecting how we create value and differentiate our products?

Generally speaking, the interactive systems used by high-ROM managers have three characteristics. First, they are simple to understand and useful for managers at many levels of the organization. Because they cascade from the top of the organization to the bottom, the importance of these measures is well understood throughout the business. Second, as we've noted, they generate information that relates to the possible outcomes of strategic uncertainties in the business. As managers scrutinize such data in face-to-face meetings, several questions recur: What has changed? Why? and What are we going to do about it? The answers create an environment that encourages managers to learn about customers, markets, technology, and other factors that may affect strategy. And finally, these systems are alive—they generate information used to revise action plans. In other words, the systems are worth the attention of managers because they can spark meaningful strategic change.

There is a corollary to Acid Test #5. It is that high-ROM managers must make sure that their employees— once they have been told and shown by example what "matters to the boss"—become the boss's eyes and ears on the front line of the business. High-ROM managers mobilize the entire organization to scan the environment for early warnings of either changes in the marketplace or competitive threats.

Equally important, employees in high-ROM organizations must routinely send new information up the line so that senior managers can use it to realign strategy. To adapt successfully in highly competitive environments, managers must signal their priorities to ensure that those employees closest to customers, technology, and markets are constantly informing top-level managers about changes that might affect the business.

Consider Intel Corporation, which in 1983 was primarily a manufacturer of dynamic random access memory (DRAM) chips. Today, Intel is known worldwide as the undisputed leader in higher value-added microprocessors. One of the most interesting aspects of this radical—and successful—change was that it emerged from the organization's middle management and operations people rather than from strategists at the top.[5]

How did that happen? Senior managers were very clear in communicating to the organization what they believed was important to succeed in the semiconductor market: efficient use of scarce production capacity. The key measure that Intel consistently used to allocate capacity was contribution margin per batch of silicon, or, in technical terms, contribution margin per wafer. Employees at all levels were well aware that senior managers frequently looked at this measure. Everyone watched what the boss watched. Therefore, it was not surprising that operational decisions started to favor microprocessors, which made a higher contribution per wafer. When senior managers became fully aware of the changing nature of Intel's business, the new direction was already becoming a reality. The fact that employees knew that senior managers were driven by contribution margin per wafer

To test ROM, ask random employees a few simple questions: What does the boss watch? Are you watching it too?

actually led the strategic change that made Intel the world leader in the semiconductor industry.

Thus one way to test ROM is to put a few simple questions to random members of the organization: What does the boss watch? Are you watching it too? And if you saw something that challenged our performance in that arena, what would you do? Whom would you tell? What information systems would provide early warning? If everyone answers these questions quickly, consistently, and accurately, managers should have no fear about their ROM. If not, it's probably time for some changes in business as usual.

High ROM: Focus and Communication

Like all business ratios, ROM is maximized by increasing the numerator (amount of productive organizational energy released) and decreasing the denominator (amount of management time and attention invested). It's time to practice what we preach. Your time is valuable, and you have read enough to understand our main point: return on management is a function of managerial focus and communication.

The energy of an organization's employees becomes most productive when they have a crystal-clear understanding of their organization's strategy. This understanding is the responsibility of managers, who can use both words and actions to communicate what people should be doing—and what they shouldn't be doing. It is inescapable that persistent and insidious forces often work against high ROM. But these forces—often rooted in good intentions—can and must be counteracted. Such is the most important work of managers.

Perhaps it is overly optimistic to call for organizational change in which all energy is productive—in which people spend their time only on initiatives aligned with strategic imperatives. But it is not unrealistic to suggest that most companies could significantly improve their ROM if they applied the five acid tests. A manager's time wouldn't become any less scarce, just more wisely spent. And maybe someday, managers will tell far fewer stories about the strategies that got away.

Return on Management (ROM): An Overview

$$\frac{\text{Productive organizational energy released}}{\text{Management time and attention invested}}$$

Managers have long used key business ratios to assess the payback from financial resources, such as assets, equity, and capital employed. Return on management (ROM) is designed to do the same for the organization's scarcest resource—its managers' time and attention. ROM measures how well managers are keeping themselves and their employees focused on strategy implementation. Like its cousins—ROCE, ROA, and the like—ROM is maximized when the numerator is large and the denominator is small or, as described below, when its allies are many and its enemies few.

The Allies of High ROM

- Clarity exists about which customers, projects, investments, or activities are out of the organization's strategic boundaries.

- Critical performance variables are selected for one purpose—to keep everyone looking over his or her shoulder in order to ensure the strategy won't fail.

- Managers know their key diagnostic measures—never more than seven at a time—by heart.

- Managerial paperwork and processes exist only where they add value to the bottom line.

- Employees know what keeps the boss awake at night and make that their business all day long.

The Enemies of High ROM

- A company has a "sky's the limit" strategy driven by vague or overly broad mission statements.

- "Politically correct" performance variables are in place that are designed not to exclude or offend any constituency in the organization.

- People are not sure what they are accountable for, or they face so many measures that they are overwhelmed.

- Planning, budgeting, and control systems have a life of their own.

- Employees have little—or no—awareness of senior management's priorities.

Notes

1. The Automation Consulting Services case study by Robert Simons and Hilary Weston (Case 9-190-053) is a synthesis derived from the experiences of several companies.

2. For complete details on ADP's strategic boundary checklist, see Robert Simons, *Levers of Control* (Harvard Business School Press, 1995), pp. 50–51.

3. George A. Miller, "The Magic Number Seven, Plus or Minus Two: Some Limits in Our Capacity for Processing Information." *The Psychological Review*, Vol. 63, No. 2, 1956, pp. 81–97.

4. John Sculley, *Odyssey: Pepsi to Apple ... A Journey of Adventure, Ideas, and the Future* (New York: Harper & Row, 1987), pp. 2, 6–7.

5. Robert A. Burgelman, "A Process Model of Strategic Business Exit: Implications for an Evolutionary Perspective on Strategy," *Strategic Management Journal*, Vol. 17, 1996, special issue, pp. 193–214.

Originally published in January–February 1998
Reprint 98110

How the Right Measures Help Teams Excel

CHRISTOPHER MEYER

Executive Summary

AT MANY COMPANIES THAT HAVE MOVED from control-oriented, functional hierarchies to faster and flatter multi-functional teams, traditional performance-measurement systems not only fail to support these teams but also undermine them, Christopher Meyer argues. Many managers fail to realize that traditional measures, which focus on results, may help them keep score on the performance of their businesses but do not help a multifunctional team monitor the activities or capabilities that enable it to perform a given process. Nor do such *results measures* tell team members what they must do to improve their performance.

How should performance-measurement systems be overhauled to maximize the effectiveness of teams? First, the overarching purpose of the system should be to help a team, rather than top managers, gauge its progress.

Next, a truly empowered team must play the lead role in designing its own measurement system. And because a team is responsible for a value-delivery process that cuts across several functions, it must create new measures to track this process. Finally, a team should adopt only a handful of measures.

Senior managers play an important role in helping teams develop performance measures by dictating strategic goals, ensuring that each team understands how it fits into those goals, and training a team to devise its own measures. But managers must never make the mistake of thinking that they know what is best for the team. If they do, they will have returned to the comand-and-control days of yore, and they will have rendered their empowered teams powerless.

MANY EXECUTIVES HAVE REALIZED that process-focused, multifunctional teams can dramatically improve the way their companies deliver products and services to customers. Most executives have not yet realized, however, that such teams need new performance-measurement systems to fulfill their promise.

The design of any performance-measurement system should reflect the basic operating assumptions of the organization it supports. If the organization changes and the measurement system doesn't, the latter will be at best ineffective or, more likely, counterproductive. At many companies that have moved from control-oriented, functional hierarchies to a faster and flatter team-based approach, traditional performance-measurement systems not only fail to support the new teams but also undermine them. Indeed, traditional systems often heighten the conflicts between multifunctional teams and functions that are vexing many organizations today.

Ideally, a measurement system designed to support a team-based organization should help teams overcome two major obstacles to their effectiveness: getting functions to provide expertise to teams when they need it and getting people from different functions on a team to speak a common language. Traditional measurement systems don't solve those problems.

The primary role of traditional measurement systems, which are still used in most companies, is to pull "good information" up so that senior managers can make "good decisions" that flow down. To that end, each relatively independent function has its own set of measures, whose main purpose is to inform top managers about its activities. Marketing tracks market share, operations watches inventory, finance monitors costs, and so on.

Such *results measures* tell an organization where it stands in its effort to achieve goals but not how it got there or, even more important, what it should do differently. Most results measures track what goes on within a function, not what happens across functions. The few cross-functional results measures in organizations are typically financial, like revenues, gross margins, costs of goods sold, capital assets, and debt, and they exist only to help top managers. In contrast, *process measures* monitor the tasks and activities throughout an organization that produce a given result. Such measures are essential for cross-functional teams that are responsible for processes that deliver an entire service or product to customers, like order fulfillment or new-product development. Unlike a traditional, functional organization, a team-based organization not only makes it possible to use process measures but also requires them.

How should performance-measurement systems be overhauled to maximize the effectiveness of teams? Here are four guiding principles:

1. The overarching purpose of a measurement system should be to help a team, rather than top managers, gauge its progress. A team's measurement system should primarily be a tool for telling the team when it must take corrective action. The measurement system must also provide top managers with a means to intervene if the team runs into problems it cannot solve by itself. But even if a team has good measures, they will be of little use if senior managers use them to control the team. A measurement system is not only the measures but also the way they are used.

2. A truly empowered team must play the lead role in designing its own measurement system. A team will know best what sort of measurement system it needs, but the team should not design this system in isolation. Senior managers must ensure that the resulting measurement system is consistent with the company's strategy.

3. Because a team is responsible for a value-delivery process that cuts across several functions (like product development, order fulfillment, or customer service), it must create measures to track that process. In a traditional functional organization, no single function is responsible for a total value-delivery process; thus there are no good ways to measure those processes. In contrast, the purpose of the multifunctional team approach is to create a structure—the team—that is responsible for a complete value-delivery process. Teams must create measures that support their mission, or they will not fully exploit their ability to perform the process faster and in a way that is more responsive to customer demands.

A process measure that a product-development team might use is one that tracks staffing levels to make sure that the necessary people are on a given team at the right time. Another measure is the number or percentage of new or unique parts to be used in a product. While such parts may offer a performance advantage, the more a product contains, the greater the likelihood that there will be difficult design, integration, inventory, manufacturing, and assembly issues.

Having sung the praises of process measures, let me throw in a qualification: while such measures are extremely important, teams still need to use some traditional measures, like one that tracks receivables, to ensure that functional and team results are achieved. Functional excellence is a prerequisite for team excellence.

4. **A team should adopt only a handful of measures.** The long-held view that "what gets measured gets done" has spurred managers to react to intensifying competition by piling more and more measures on their operations in a bid to encourage employees to work harder. As a result, team members end up spending too much time collecting data and monitoring their activities and not enough time managing the project. I have seen dozens of teams spend too much time at meetings discussing the mechanics of the measurement system instead of discussing what to *do*. As a general rule, if a team has

Trying to run a team without a good, simple guidance system is like trying to drive a car without a dashboard.

more than 15 measures, it should take a fresh look at the importance of each one.

Trying to run a team without a good, simple guidance system is like trying to drive a car without a dashboard. We might do it in a pinch but not as a matter of practice, because we'd lack the necessary information—the speed, the amount of fuel, the engine temperature—to ensure that we reach our destination. Companies may find it helpful to create a computerized "dashboard," which inexpensive graphics software has made easy to do. (See "The Team Dashboard, " on page 114.)

The lack of an effective measurement system, or dashboard, can even prevent teams from making it much past the starting line. After companies first adopt the team approach, teams must typically prove to skeptical senior and middle managers that the power these managers have wielded can be handed to the teams without the business spinning out of control. A team can offer no such proof if it lacks the tools to track its performance.

What operations executive, for example, would be willing to let a new-product development team manage the transition from an existing product to a new one if the team did not have a measure that tracked old product inventory from the factory throughout the distribution channel? Without such information, the company might end up stuck with lots of an unsellable old product. And what development executive would be willing to hand over responsibility for a project if he or she did not see that the product-development team was able to track cost, quality, and schedule?

MANY MANAGERS FAIL TO REALIZE that results measures like profits, market share, and cost, which may help them keep score on the performance of their businesses, do not help a multifunctional team, or any organization, monitor the activities or capabilities that enable it to perform a given process. Nor do such measures tell team members what they must do to improve their performance.

An 8% drop in quarterly profits accompanied by a 10% rise in service costs, for example, does not tell a customer-service team what its service technicians should do differently on their next call. Process measures, however, examine the actions and capabilities that contributed to the situation. Knowing that the average time spent per service call rose 15% last month and that, as a result, the number of late calls rose 10% would explain to the technicians why service costs had gone up and customer satisfaction and profits had gone down.

The fact that a program is six months late and $2 million over budget doesn't tell anyone what went wrong or what to do next.

The most commonly used results measures in product development are schedule and cost. But the fact that a program is six months late and $2 million over budget doesn't tell anyone what went wrong or what to do differently. In contrast, tracking staffing levels during the course of a project—a process measure that might include not only the number of bodies but also the years of experience in major job categories—can radically affect a team's performance. Many product-development teams, for example, do a poor job planning exactly when they will need people with a certain functional expertise. Not having all the necessary people at a particular stage often leads to expensive and time-consuming efforts to fix problems that the right people would have detected earlier.

This is exactly what I saw happen at a company that had given a multifunctional team seven months to develop a consumer product for testing blood-sugar levels. The team began work on July 1 and had a February 1 target date for launching the product. Although the company had named the people from the critical functions who would serve on the team well before the effort got under way, Mary, the manufacturing representative, did not join the team until mid-August. By then, people from marketing and development engineering had already made some best-guess decisions about significant packaging and manufacturing issues. After one week on the team, Mary raised serious questions about many of those decisions, and the team decided to adopt her suggestions and retrace its steps. Not only was Mary's arrival on the team very awkward, but also the program slipped by three weeks within the first two months.

A team's reliance on traditional measures can also cause its members to forget the team's goal and revert to their old functional way of working—or fighting—with one another. Consider the case of Ford Motor Company during the development of a luxury model in 1991. The project was one of Ford's first attempts to use multifunctional teams for product development. By and large, the team's measurement system was a collection of the individual measures that each function on the team (styling, body engineering, power train, purchasing, finance, etc.) had used for years.

Shortly before team members were to sign off on the car's design and begin engineering the body, a controversy developed over the door handle, which was different from the ones Ford had been using. One reason for the controversy was that each function made different assumptions about the relative importance of the factors contributing to the product's costs and competitiveness.

Members from the purchasing and finance departments feared that the handle would be too expensive. Their gauges were the cost of manufacturing the handle and its warranty costs. The people from design and body engineering responded that the handle's design was no more complex than that of existing handles. And because there was no basis for assuming that its warranty costs would be higher, they argued, the cost of manufacturing the handle should be the main issue in the cost debate. They submitted a bid from a vendor on Ford's approved vendor list as proof that the handle would be no more expensive to make. In addition, they argued, purchasing and finance were not giving enough weight to the importance of the handle's design in the overall design of the car.

The purchasing representative was still not satisfied about the warranty costs. He said that handles made by other approved vendors had had lower warranty costs than handles made by the vendor whose bid had been submitted. After a short shouting match, the design and engineering people gave up.

During the debate, no one asked the critical question: Would the new handle increase the car's ability to compete in the marketplace? Since the model's distinctive styling was a critical competitive element, the new handle might have helped the vehicle capture enough additional customers to more than compensate for higher warranty costs. Adopting the old handle was not necessarily the best decision, and this last-minute design change, which in turn required other changes, added at least one week to the development process. The members of this product-development team were still thinking as they did in their functions, where nobody had an overview of what would make the product succeed in the marketplace.

What kind of measures could have helped the team avoid its win-lose battle over cost versus style? One possibility would have been a measure that incorporated several product attributes, such as product cost, features, service, and packaging, to enable the team to assess trade-offs. This may have helped the team realize that an undetermined factor—the proposed handle's warranty costs—should not have influenced the decision so heavily.

Top managers must set strategic goals, show a team how it fits into those goals, and train the team to choose its own measures.

WHEN CROSS-FUNCTIONAL TEAMS ARE BEING ESTABLISHED, many companies do not institute a measurement system that supports the company's strategy, ensures senior managers that there won't be unpleasant surprises, and, last but not least, truly empowers the teams. Let me offer a generic process that most companies can implement. I'll start with the role of top managers.

In two articles on the *balanced scorecard* ("The Balanced Scorecard—Measures that Drive Performance," on page 123, and "Putting the Balanced Scorecard to Work," on page 147), Robert S. Kaplan and David P. Norton provide managers with a valuable framework for integrating a company's strategic objectives and competitive demands into its performance-measurement system. They urge managers to augment their traditional financial measures with measures of customer satisfaction, internal processes, and innovation and improvement activities.

What Kaplan and Norton do not explain is how such an approach can be applied to team-based organizations. I believe that it can, with one caveat: senior managers should create the strategic context for the teams but not the measures. Senior managers should dictate strategic goals, ensure that each team understands how its job fits into the strategy, and provide training so that the team can devise its own measures. But to ensure that ownership of and accountability for performance remains with the teams, managers must require the teams to decide which measures will best help them perform their jobs.

For example, the managers of a multinational computer company established an ambitious strategic goal for all of the company's product-development teams to reduce their cycle times by more than 50% within three years. But rather than dictating how the teams measure cycle time, managers asked each team to select its own measures. To help the teams in this effort, managers provided training in cycle-time reduction and a very broad selection of measures from which the teams could choose.

Top managers and a team should jointly establish rules about when or under what circumstances managers will review the team's performance and its measurement system. A team should know at the outset that it will have to review the measures it has selected with top managers to ensure that they are consistent with corporate strategy and that it may have to adjust its measures. The team should also promise to renegotiate with managers any major changes in the measures made during the course of the project. As I will discuss later, measures should not be carved in stone.

The team and senior managers should also set boundaries, which, if crossed, will signal that the team has run into trouble serious enough to trigger an "out-of-bounds" management review. Such an approach keeps managers informed without disenfranchising the team.

During an out-of-bounds review, teams and managers must define the problem and decide what corrective action to take. The team must retain responsibility for calling and running the review and executing any decisions. It must be clear that the purpose of the reviews is for senior managers to help the teams solve problems, not to find fault.

Some product-development teams actually negotiate written contracts with senior managers at the start of a project. The contracts define the product, including features and quality targets; the targeted cost to the customer; the program cost; financial information like revenues, gross margins, and cost of goods sold; and the schedule. During the contract negotiations, management ensures that the overall program, including the measures, supports the company's strategy.

The contract also establishes rules for management reviews. For example, one company requires only two planned reviews. The first comes at the end of the design phase so that management can confirm that the product still meets the market need before the company invests in expensive tooling. The second review is after production is under way so that management can learn about and pass on to other teams any advances that the team has made, like designing a particular component to be manufactured easily, and can solve unforeseen production problems early on. During the entire design phase, the team is free to proceed without any contact with management unless it has broken or knows it will break its commitments on product features, performance, product and development costs, or schedule.

The main problem at most companies that now use multifunctional teams is that top managers use a team's measurement system to monitor and control projects or processes. Even if unintentional, such behavior will inevitably undermine the effectiveness of any team.

This is what happened when a Ford manufacturing plant turned to multifunctional teams to improve product quality but didn't change management's command-and-control mind-set.

The company grouped line workers from various functional areas into teams and trained them to collect and analyze data so that they could resolve quality problems on their own. But then came the mistake: the division managers asked quality engineers, who supposedly had been sent to assist the teams, to send a monthly report on the plant's quality and plans for improving it. In turn, the quality engineers asked the teams for their data.

Over time, the teams began to depend on the quality engineers to analyze the data and waited for the engineers' directions before taking action. The engineers recognized what was happening but felt caught in a bind because the division managers wanted them, rather than the teams, to provide the reports. Problems that the teams had been able to resolve on their own in a day or two began to require the involvement of the quality engineers and twice the time. And the quality engineers asked for more engineers to help them support the teams.

The division managers became very frustrated. Given all their verbal support for empowering teams, they couldn't understand why the teams didn't act empowered.

WHEN A GROUP OF PEOPLE BUILDS A MEASURE-
MENT SYSTEM, it also builds a team. One benefit of
having a team create its own measurement system is
that members who hail from different functions end up
creating a common language, which they need in order
to work as an effective team. Until a group creates a
common language, it can't reach a common definition of
goals or problems. Instead of acting like a team, the
group will act like a collection of functions.

As a first step, the team should develop a work plan
that can serve as a process map of the critical tasks and
capabilities required to complete the project. The second step is to make sure that everyone understands the
team's goals in the same way. Team members frequently
start out believing that they share an understanding of
their goals only to discover when they begin developing
performance measures how wrong they were.

After the goals have been confirmed, the appropriate
team members should develop individual measures for
gauging the team's progress in achieving a given goal
and identifying the conditions that would trigger an out-
of-bounds review. In addition, each member should
come to the next meeting with two or three gauges that
he or she considers most effective for monitoring his or
her functional area. In an attempt to push team members to focus on overall goals and the total value-delivery
process as they develop measures, they should be
encouraged to include process measures. (See "Creating
Process Measures, " on page 120.)

At the next meeting, each member should explain
what his or her proposed measures track and why they
are important. Everyone should make an effort to define
any terms or concepts that are unfamiliar to others. One
important rule is that no question is a "dumb question."

So-called dumb questions are often the most valuable because they test the potential value of each measure in the most obvious terms.

Some measures will be either eliminated or agreed on very quickly. The hard work will be assessing those that fall in between. No final decisions should be made until all the gauges accepted or still in contention are tested as a unit against the following criteria:

- Are critical team objectives (like filling an order within 24 hours) tracked?

- Are all out-of-bounds conditions monitored?

- Are the critical variables required to reach the goal (like having enough skilled personnel to run an order-entry system) tracked?

- Would management approve the system as is or seek changes?

- Is there any gauge that wouldn't cause the team to change its behavior if the needle swung from one side to another? If so, eliminate it.

- Are there too many gauges? As I mentioned earlier, if a team has more than 15 measures, it should take a second look at each one.

After a team's measures have passed this test, the system is ready for the management review.

A TEAM CAN PRESERVE THE VALUE of its performance-measurement system by diligently adding and eliminating gauges, as required, during the project or task.

Measures that were relevant during the early stages in the development of a new product will undoubtedly become irrelevant as the product nears production. In most cases, teams realize that and plan for changes during the development of their measurement systems. But priorities often change during a project, which means that measures should be changed too. And sometimes measures prove not to be so useful after all and should be dropped. A team should also regularly audit the data being fed into its measurement system to make sure they are accurate and timely.

Managers are still in the early stages of learning how to maximize the effectiveness of multifunctional teams that are incorporated into their functional organizations. The same applies to the measurement systems used to guide both. As companies gain experience, they will discover that some specific measures can be used over and over again by different teams undertaking similar tasks or projects. But managers should be on their guard lest they do with performance-measurement systems what they have done with so many management tools: assume that one size fits all. Managers can systematize the process that teams use to create their measurement systems. They can also catalog the measures that appear to have been most effective in particular applications. But managers must never make the mistake of thinking that they know what is best for the team. If they do, they will have crossed the line and returned to the command-and-control ways of yore. And they will have rendered their empowered teams powerless.

The Team Dashboard

SPREADSHEETS ARE THE MOST COMMON FORMAT companies use to display their performance measures.

But if a measurement system should function like a car's dashboard by providing a multifunctional team with the information it needs to complete its journey, why not actually construct a dashboard? The dashboard format, complete with colorful graphic indicators and other easy-to-read gauges, makes it much easier for a team to monitor its progress and know when it must change direction. A multifunctional team called Lethal, which designed and built a 2.5-inch disk drive for the Quantum Corporation in Milpitas, California, used the displayed dashboard.

Quantum had begun using multifunctional development teams only nine months before it established the Lethal team late in 1989. Lethal's core group included representatives from marketing, manufacturing, engineering, quality assurance, finance, and human resources. While Quantum was a strong player in the 3.5-inch drive segment, it had never made 2.5-inch drives. On top of this technical challenge, managers wanted Lethal to deliver the drive in 14 months—10 months less than similar projects had taken.

Larry, the team's principal leader, who came from engineering, was very skeptical about whether or not Quantum's past development practices would enable Lethal to reach its 14-month goal. When he asked leaders from previous teams what they would do differently, all said they would try to find a better way to detect problems early. The teams would gather all the right players, but too many problems still ended up being resolved in the functions. Larry recognized one reason for that situation: the teams had used measurement systems designed for hierarchical, functional organizations. He thought Lethal could do better.

When the team began trying to establish a schedule, its members quickly discovered that development engineering was the only function that had provided a complete schedule for performing its tasks. The others had only sketched out major milestones. In addition, individual team members were often unsure what the others' schedules meant, and none of the schedules had been integrated. Marketing had even gone ahead and set a date for the product launch without consulting development engineering!

After this revelation, the team members decided to spell out the details of all the functional schedules in terms that everyone could understand. They then integrated those schedules into one master product-development schedule, which product-development programs often lack.

In addition to this schedule monitor and a milestone gauge, the dashboard contains a variety of other results measures, which development teams typically use to track their progress in achieving the key strategic goals that will determine whether or not top managers consider the project a success. Lethal's goals included creating a product that could be manufactured at a targeted cost (tracked by the "Overhead" and "Bills of Materials" gauges) and had a competitive quality level (tracked by the "Product Quality" gauge). The dashboard also has results measures for tracking the product's success in achieving profit margin and revenue targets once it is on the market. But such results measures tell a team only where it stands, not why it stands there. To do the latter, Lethal adopted the first process measures used by multifunctional teams in the company.

Previous teams at Quantum had focused on developing the product and treated as secondary such tasks as developing the methods and equipment for testing. Only after teams discovered that early prototypes couldn't be adequately tested did those issues receive attention. To avoid such a bottleneck, Lethal adopted a separate process-development gauge for all the tasks involved in manufacturing, including testing.

A similar discussion resulted in a decision to include staffing gauges on the dashboard. People for areas like testing, manufacturing, and marketing had to be hired early enough so that they would be on board when the team needed them. If the team waited until the development of testing methods and equipment were supposed to start before hiring test engineers, the schedule could slip by at least six weeks.

Larry's motive for suggesting the employee-satisfaction gauge was simple: unhappy team members won't keep to an ambitious schedule. The position of the "Current" needle reflects the team leaders' opinion of the team's morale. The position of the "Last survey" needle reflects the most recent survey of all team members. By forcing themselves to monitor morale, the leaders discovered that people were concerned about such things as the shortage of lab space and access to the workstations and were able to do something about those issues before they hurt morale.

The indicator lights in the lower left-hand corner of the dashboard were designed to ensure that the team allocated enough time to planning. While weekly team meetings were adequate for dealing with many issues, some, like product-launch planning, required more preparation. Because of the program's intensity, team members worried that issues that couldn't be solved quickly would eventually cause a bottleneck. Scheduling a half- or full-day meeting that everyone could attend would often take at least four weeks. John from marketing suggested that the team use the indicator lights as a reminder to schedule time for planning sessions.

The team quickly realized which gauges were not useful. John from finance argued that determining Lethal's expenses for the "Program Cost to Date" gauge was nearly impossible since the company did not have a project-based accounting system. Moreover, top

---

Lethal's Dashboard

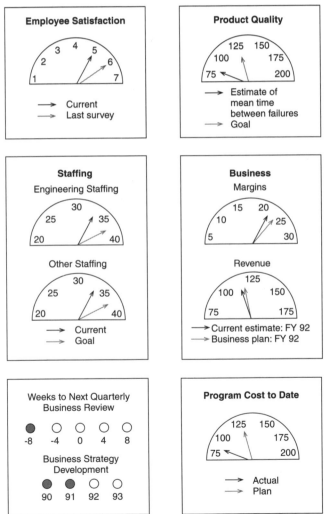

managers rarely asked about an individual program's costs because they hardly varied from project to project. Since nobody on the team changed his or her behavior if the program-cost gauge dropped or increased, the team decided to eliminate it.

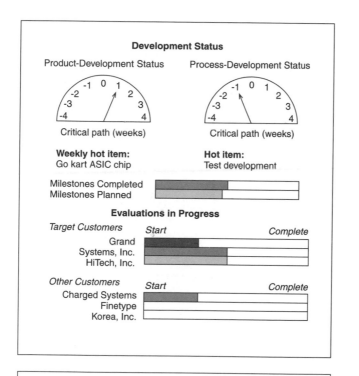

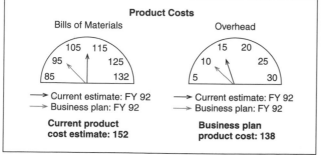

The team succeeded in getting potential customers for the 2.5-inch disk drive to approve the company as a qualified supplier in 16 months—2 months over the original target date but still 33% faster than previous teams. However, the drive took longer to move through the actual qualification phase than previous drives. The "Evaluations in Progress" gauges helped Lethal track its progress with potential customers but did not help the team discover a key problem until relatively late: Lethal's test procedures were more rigorous than those used by potential customers, which made it look as if the drives' failure rate was relatively high. On the basis of these data, potential customers would not qualify the company as a supplier.

Could a dashboard with different gauges have detected the problem early enough to solve it? Probably not. Like any performance-measurement tool, the dashboard is not a replacement for the decision maker.

Creating Process Measures

THERE ARE FOUR BASIC STEPS to creating process measures: defining what kinds of factors, such as time, cost, quality, and product performance, are critical to satisfying customers; mapping the cross-functional process used to deliver results; identifying the critical tasks and capabilities required to complete the process successfully; and, finally, designing measures that track those tasks and capabilities. The most effective process measures are often those that express relative terms. For example, a measure that tracks the percentage of new or unique parts is usually more valuable than one that tracks the absolute number.

Here's how the parts and service operation of a Europe-based car company created process measures.

The warehousing function had traditionally measured its performance by tracking how often parts ordered by dealers could be filled immediately from the warehouse shelf. If a stock picker found a gasket on the warehouse shelf—meaning that it did not have to be ordered—that counted as a "first fill."

When the organization began using teams, it put the warehousing and the dealer-service groups on a multi-functional team charged with improving the total service process, from product breakdown through repair. The team reexamined the current performance measures and concluded that, from the dealer's perspective, the first-fill measure was meaningless. Dealers—and the final customers—didn't care where the part came from; they just wanted to know when they'd receive it. And just because a part was on the warehouse shelf did not ensure that it would get to a dealer quickly; the sloppy handling of orders and shipping problems could also cause delays.

Because the new team was responsible for the entire process, it mapped all the steps in the service cycle, from the moment the warehouse received a dealer's order to the moment the dealer received the part, and the time each step took. The team then identified its critical tasks and capabilities, which included the order-entry operation, the management-information system for tracking orders and inventories, warehouse operations, and shipping. The team created cycle-time measures for six to eight sub-processes, which helped the team see how much time was being spent on each step of the process relative to the value of that process. With this information, the team could begin figuring out how to reduce cycle time without sacrificing quality. The resulting changes included reducing the copies made of each order and the number of signatures required to authorize filling it. Within six months, the team was able to reduce the service cycle considerably. Not coincidentally, dealer complaints fell by a comparable amount.

Originally published in May–June 1994
Reprint 94305

The author would like to thank Steven C. Wheelwright, who provided valuable guidance for this article.

The Balanced Scorecard— Measures that Drive Performance

ROBERT S. KAPLAN AND DAVID P. NORTON

Executive Summary

FRUSTRATED BY THE INADEQUACIES OF TRADITIONAL PERFORMANCE MEASUREMENT SYSTEMS, some managers have abandoned financial measures like return on equity and earnings per share. "Make operational improvements and the numbers will follow," the argument goes. But managers do not want to choose between financial and operational measures. Executives want a balanced presentation of measures that allow them to view the company from several perspectives simultaneously.

During a year-long research project with 12 companies at the leading edge of performance measurement, the authors developed a "balanced scorecard," a new performance measurement system that gives top managers a fast but comprehensive view of the business. The balanced scorecard includes financial measures that tell the results of actions already taken. And it complements those financial measure with three sets of operational measures having to do with customer satisfaction, internal processes, and the organization's ability to learn and improve—the activities that drive future financial performance.

Managers can create a balanced scorecard by translating their company's strategy and mission statements into specific goals and measures. To create the part of the scorecard that focuses on the customer perspective, for example, executives at Electronic Circuits Inc. established general goals for customer performance: get standard products to market sooner, improve customers' time-to-market, become customers' supplier of choice through partnerships, and develop innovative products tailored to customer needs. Managers translated these elements of strategy into four specific goals and identified a measure for each.

WHAT YOU MEASURE IS WHAT YOU GET. Senior executives understand that their organization's measurement system strongly affects the behavior of managers and employees. Executives also understand that traditional financial accounting measures like return-on-investment and earnings-per-share can give misleading signals for continuous improvement and innovation—activities today's competitive environment demands. The traditional financial performance measures worked well for the industrial era, but they are out of step with the skills and competencies companies are trying to master today.

As managers and academic researchers have tried to remedy the inadequacies of current performance measurement systems, some have focused on making financial measures more relevant. Others have said, "Forget the financial measures. Improve operational measures like cycle time and defect rates; the financial results will follow." But managers should not have to choose between financial and operational measures. In observing and working with many companies, we have found that senior executives do not rely on one set of measures to the exclusion of the other. They realize that no single measure can provide a clear performance target or focus attention on the critical areas of the business. Managers want a balanced presentation of both financial and operational measures.

During a year-long research project with 12 companies at the leading edge of performance measurement, we devised a "balanced scorecard"—a set of measures that gives top managers a fast but comprehensive view of the business. The balanced scorecard includes financial measures that tell the results of actions already taken. And it complements the financial measures with operational measures on customer satisfaction, internal processes, and the organization's innovation and improvement activities—operational measures that are the drivers of future financial performance.

The balanced scorecard is like the dials in an airplane cockpit: it give managers complex information at a glance.

Think of the balanced scorecard as the dials and indicators in an airplane cockpit. For the complex task of navigating and flying an airplane, pilots need detailed information about many aspects of the flight. They need information on fuel, air speed, altitude, bearing, destination, and other indicators that summarize the current and predicted environment. Reliance on one instrument can be fatal. Similarly, the complexity of managing an organization today requires that managers be able to view performance in several areas simultaneously.

The balanced scorecard allows managers to look at the business from four important perspectives (See the exhibit "The Balanced Scorecard Links Performance Measures.") It provides answers to four basic questions:

- How do customers see us? (customer perspective)

- What must we excel at? (internal perspective)

- Can we continue to improve and create value? (innovation and learning perspective)

- How do we look to shareholders? (financial perspective)

While giving senior managers information from four different perspectives, the balanced scorecard minimizes information overload by limiting the number of measures used. Companies rarely suffer from having too few measures. More commonly, they keep adding new measures whenever an employee or a consultant makes a worthwhile suggestion. One manager described the proliferation of new measures at his company as its "kill another tree program." The balanced scorecard forces managers to focus on the handful of measures that are most critical.

The balanced scorecard shows **how** *results are achieved: Did the cost of setups fall because of shorter setup times or bigger batch sizes?*

Several companies have already adopted the balanced scorecard. Their early experiences using the scorecard have demonstrated that it meets several managerial needs. First, the scorecard brings together, in a single management report, many of the seemingly disparate elements of a company's competitive agenda: becoming customer oriented, shortening response time, improving quality, emphasizing teamwork, reducing new product launch times, and managing for the long term.

Second, the scorecard guards against suboptimization. By forcing senior managers to consider all the important operational measures together, the balanced scorecard lets them see whether improvement in one area may have been achieved at the expense of another. Even the best objective can be achieved badly. Compa-

The Balanced Scorecard Links Performance Measures

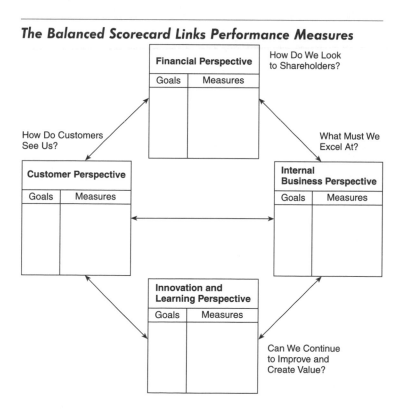

nies can reduce time to market, for example, in two very different ways: by improving the management of new product introductions or by releasing only products that are incrementally different from existing products. Spending on setups can be cut either by reducing setup times or by increasing batch sizes. Similarly, production output and first-pass yields can rise, but the increases may be due to a shift in the product mix to more standard, easy-to-produce but lower-margin products.

We will illustrate how companies can create their own balanced scorecard with the experiences of one semiconductor company—let's call it Electronic Circuits Inc. ECI saw the scorecard as a way to clarify, simplify, and then operationalize the vision at the top of the organization. The ECI scorecard was designed to focus the attention of its top executives on a short list of critical indicators of current and future performance.

Customer Perspective: How Do Customers See Us?

Many companies today have a corporate mission that focuses on the customer. "To be number one in delivering value to customers" is a typical mission statement. How a company is performing from its customers' perspective has become, therefore, a priority for top management. The balanced scorecard demands that managers translate their general mission statement on customer service into specific measures that reflect the factors that really matter to customers.

Customers' concerns tend to fall into four categories: time, quality, performance and service, and cost. Lead time measures the time required for the company to meet its customers' needs. For existing products, lead time can be measured from the time the company receives an order to the time it actually delivers the product or service to the customer. For new products, lead time represents the time to market, or how long it takes to bring a new product from the product definition stage to the start of shipments. Quality measures the defect level of incoming products as perceived and measured by the customer. Quality could also measure on-time delivery, the accuracy of the company's delivery forecasts. The combination of performance and service measures how the company's products or services contribute to creating value for its customers. (See "Other Measures for the Customer's Perspective," on page 141.)

To put the balanced scorecard to work, companies should articulate goals for time, quality, and performance and service and then translate these goals into specific measures. Senior managers at ECI, for example, established general goals for customer performance: get standard products to market sooner, improve customers' time to market, become customers' supplier of choice through partnerships with them, and develop innovative products tailored to customer needs. The managers translated these general goals into four specific goals and identified an appropriate measure for each. (See the exhibit "ECI's Balanced Scorecard.")

To track the specific goal of providing a continuous stream of attractive solutions, ECI measured the percent of sales from new products and the percent of sales from proprietary products. That information was available internally. But certain other measures forced the company to get data from outside. To assess whether the company was achieving its goal of providing reliable, responsive supply, ECI turned to its customers. When it found that each customer defined "reliable, responsive

supply" differently, ECI created a database of the factors
as defined by each of its major customers. The shift to
external measures of performance with customers led
ECI to redefine "on time" so it matched customers'
expectations. Some customers defined "on-time" as any
shipment that arrived within five days of scheduled
delivery; others used a nine-day window. ECI itself had
been using a seven-day window, which meant that the
company was not satisfying some of its customers and

ECI's Balanced Business Scorecard

Financial Perspective		Customer Perspective	
Goals	Measures	Goals	Measures
Survive	Cash flow	New products	Percent of sales from new products
Succeed	Quarterly sales growth and operating income by division		Percent of sales from proprietary products
Prosper	Increased market share and ROE	Responsive supply	On-time delivery (defined by customer)
		Preferred supplier	Share of key accounts' purchases
			Ranking by key accounts
		Customer partnership	Number of cooperative engineering efforts

Internal Business Perspective		Innovation and Learning Perspective	
Goals	Measures	Goals	Measures
Technology capability	Manufacturing geometry vs. competition	Technology leadership	Time to develop next generation
Manufacturing excellence	Cycle time	Manufacturing learning	Process time to maturity
	Unit cost		
	Yield	Product focus	Percent of products that equals 80% sales
Design productivity	Silicon efficiency		
	Engineering efficiency	Time to market	New product introduction vs. competition
New product introduction	Actual introduction schedule vs. plan		

overachieving at others. ECI also asked its top ten customers to rank the company as a supplier overall.

Depending on customers' evaluations to define some of a company's performance measures forces that company to view its performance through customers' eyes. Some companies hire third parties to perform anonymous customer surveys, resulting in a customer-driven report card. The J.D. Powers quality survey, for example, has become the standard of performance for the automobile industry, while the Department of Transportation's measurement of on-time arrivals and lost baggage provides external standards for airlines. Benchmarking procedures are yet another technique companies use to compare their performance against competitors' best practice. Many companies have introduced "best of breed" comparison programs: the company looks to one industry to find, say, the best distribution system, to another industry for the lowest cost payroll process, and then forms a composite of those best practices to set objectives for its own performance.

In addition to measures of time, quality, and performance and service, companies must remain sensitive to the cost of their products. But customers see price as only one component of the cost they incur when dealing with their suppliers. Other supplier-driven costs range from ordering, scheduling delivery, and paying for the materials; to receiving, inspecting, handling, and storing the materials; to the scrap, rework, and obsolescence caused by the materials; and schedule disruptions (expediting and value of lost output) from incorrect deliveries. An excellent supplier may charge a higher unit price for products than other vendors but nonetheless be a lower cost supplier because it can deliver defect-free products in exactly the right quantities at exactly the right time directly to the production process and can minimize, through electronic data interchange, the administrative hassles of ordering, invoicing, and paying for materials.

Internal Business Perspective: What Must We Excel at?

Customer-based measures are important, but they must be translated into measures of what the company must do internally to meet its customers' expectations. After all, excellent customer performance derives from processes, decisions, and actions occurring throughout an organization. Managers need to focus on those critical internal operations that enable them to satisfy customer needs. The second part of the balanced scorecard gives managers that internal perspective.

The internal measures for the balanced scorecard should stem from the business processes that have the greatest impact on customer satisfaction—factors that affect cycle time, quality, employee skills, and productivity, for example. Companies should also attempt to identify and measure their company's core competencies, the critical technologies needed to ensure continued market leadership. Companies should decide what processes and competencies they must excel at and specify measures for each. (See "Other Measures for the Internal Business Perspective," on page 142.)

Managers at ECI determined that submicron technology capability was critical to its market position. They also decided that they had to focus on manufacturing excellence, design productivity, and new product introduction. The company developed operational measures for each of these four internal business goals.

To achieve goals on cycle time, quality, productivity, and cost, managers must devise measures that are influenced by employees' actions. Since much of the action takes place at the department and workstation levels, managers need to decompose overall cycle time, quality, product, and cost measures to local levels. That way, the measures link top management's judgment about key internal processes and competencies to the actions taken by individuals that affect overall corporate objectives. This linkage ensures that employees at lower levels in the organization have clear targets for actions, decisions, and improvement activities that will contribute to the company's overall mission.

Information systems play an invaluable role in helping managers disaggregate the summary measures. When an unexpected signal appears on the balanced scorecard, executives can query their information system to find the source of the trouble. If the aggregate measure for on-time delivery is poor, for example, executives with a good information system can quickly look behind the aggregate measure until they can identify late deliveries, day by day, by a particular plant to an individual customer.

If the information system is unresponsive, however, it can be the Achilles' heel of performance measurement. Managers at ECI are currently limited by the absence of such an operational information system. Their greatest concern is that the scorecard information is not timely; reports are generally a week behind the company's routine management meetings, and the measures have yet to be linked to measures for managers and employees at lower levels of the organization. The company is in the process of developing a more responsive information system to eliminate this constraint.

Innovation and Learning Perspective: Can We Continue to Improve and Create Value?

The customer-based and internal business process measures on the balanced scorecard identify the parameters that the company considers most important for competitive success. But the targets for success keep changing. Intense global competition requires that companies make continual improvements to their *existing* products and processes and have the ability to introduce entirely new products with expanded capabilities.

A company's ability to innovate, improve, and learn ties directly to the company's value. That is, only through the ability to launch new products, create more value for customers, and improve operating efficiencies continually can a company penetrate new markets and increase revenues and margins—in short, grow and thereby increase shareholder value.

ECI's innovation measures focus on the company's ability to develop and introduce standard products rapidly, products that the company expects will form the bulk of its future sales. Its manufacturing improvement measure focuses on new products; the goal is to achieve stability in the manufacturing of new products rather than to improve manufacturing of existing products. Like many other companies, ECI uses the percent of sales from new products as one of its innovation and improvement measures. If sales from new products are trending downward, managers can explore whether problems have arisen in new product design or new product introduction.

In addition to measures on product and process innovation, some companies overlay specific improvement goals for their existing processes. For example,

Analog Devices, a Massachusetts-based manufacturer of specialized semiconductors, expects managers to improve their customer and internal business process performance continuously. The company estimates specific rates of improvement for on-time delivery, cycle time, defect rate, and yield.

Other companies, like Milliken & Co., require that managers make improvements within a specific time period. Milliken did not want its "associates" (Milliken's word for employees) to rest on their laurels after winning the Baldridge Award. Chairman and CEO Roger Milliken asked each plant to implement a "ten-four" improvement program: measures of process defects, missed deliveries, and scrap were to be reduced by a factor of ten over the next four years. These targets emphasize the role for continuous improvement in customer satisfaction and internal business processes.

Financial Perspective: How Do We Look to Shareholders?

Financial performance measures indicate whether the company's strategy, implementation, and execution are contributing to bottom-line improvement. Typical financial goals have to do with profitability, growth, and shareholder value. ECI stated its financial goals simply: to survive, to succeed, and to prosper. Survival was measured by cash flow, success by quarterly sales growth and operating income by division, and prosperity by increased market share by segment and return on equity.

But given today's business environment, should senior managers even look at the business from a financial perspective? Should they pay attention to short-term financial measures like quarterly sales and operating income? Many have criticized financial measures because of their well-documented inadequacies, their backward-looking focus, and their inability to reflect contemporary value-creating actions. Shareholder value analysis (SVA), which forecasts future cash flows and discounts them back to a rough estimate of current value, is an attempt to make financial analysis more forward looking. But SVA still is based on cash flow rather than on the activities and processes that drive cash flow.

Some critics go much further in their indictment of financial measures. They argue that the terms of competition have changed and that traditional financial measures do not improve customer satisfaction, quality, cycle time, and employee motivation. In their view, financial performance is the result of operational actions, and financial success should be the logical consequence of doing the fundamentals well. In other words, companies should stop navigating by financial measures. By making fundamental improvements in their operations, the financial numbers will take care of themselves, the argument goes.

Assertions that financial measures are unnecessary are incorrect for at least two reasons. A well-designed financial control system can actually enhance rather than inhibit an organization's total quality management program. (See "How One Company Used a Daily Financial Report to Improve Quality," on page 143.) More important, however, the alleged linkage between improved operating performance and financial success is actually quite tenuous and uncertain. Let us demonstrate rather than argue this point.

Over the three-year period between 1987 and 1990, a NYSE electronics company made an order-of-magnitude improvement in quality and on-time delivery performance. Outgoing defect rate dropped from 500 parts per million to 50, on-time delivery improved from 70% to 96% and yield jumped from 26% to 51%. Did these breakthrough improvements in quality, productivity, and customer service provide substantial benefits to the company? Unfortunately not. During the same three-year period, the company's financial results showed little improvement, and its stock price plummeted to one-third of its July 1987 value. The considerable improvements in manufacturing capabilities had not been translated into increased profitability. Slow releases of new products and a failure to expand marketing to new and perhaps more demanding customers prevented the company from realizing the benefits of its manufacturing achievements. The operational achievements were real, but the company had failed to capitalize on them.

The disparity between improved operational performance and disappointing financial measures creates frustration for senior executives. This frustration is often vented at nameless Wall Street analysts who allegedly cannot see past quarterly blips in financial performance to the underlying long-term values these executives sincerely believe they are creating in their organizations. But the hard truth is that if improved performance fails to be reflected in the bottom line, executives should reexamine the basic assumptions of their strategy and mission. Not all long-term strategies are profitable strategies.

Measures of customer satisfaction, internal business performance, and innovation and improvement are derived from the company's particular view of the world and its perspective on key success factors. But that view is not necessarily correct. Even an excellent set of balanced scorecard measures does not guarantee a winning strategy. The balanced scorecard can only translate a company's strategy into specific measurable objectives. A failure to convert improved operational performance, as measured in the scorecard, into improved financial performance should send executives back to their drawing boards to rethink the company's strategy or its implementation plans.

As one example, disappointing financial measures sometimes occur because companies don't follow up their operational improvements with another round of actions. Quality and cycle-time improvements can create excess capacity. Managers should be prepared to either put the excess capacity to work or else get rid of it. The excess capacity must be either used by boosting revenues or eliminated by reducing expenses if operational improvements are to be brought down to the bottom line.

As companies improve their quality and response time, they eliminate the need to build, inspect, and rework out-of-conformance products or to reschedule and expedite delayed orders. Eliminating these tasks means that some of the people who perform them are no longer needed. Companies are understandably reluctant to lay off employees, especially since the employees may have been the source of the ideas that produced the higher quality and reduced cycle time. Layoffs are a poor reward for past improvement and can damage the morale of remaining workers, curtailing further improvement. But companies will not realize all the financial benefits of their improvements until their employees and facilities are working to capacity—or the companies confront the pain of downsizing to eliminate the expenses of the newly created excess capacity.

If executives fully understood the consequences of their quality and cycle-time improvement programs, they might be more aggressive about using the newly created capacity. To capitalize on this self-created new capacity, however, companies must expand sales to existing customers, market existing products to entirely new customers (who are now accessible because of the improved quality and delivery performance), and increase the flow of new products to the market. These actions can generate added revenues with only modest increases in operating expenses. If marketing and sales and R&D do not generate the increased volume, the operating improvements will stand as excess capacity, redundancy, and untapped capabilities. Periodic financial statements remind executives that improved quality, response time, productivity, or new products benefit the company only when they are translated into improved sales and market share, reduced operating expenses, or higher asset turnover.

The balanced scorecard puts strategy—not control—at the center.

Ideally, companies should specify how improvements in quality, cycle time, quoted lead times, delivery, and new product introduction will lead to higher market share, operating margins, and asset turnover or to reduced operating expenses. The challenge is to learn how to make such explicit linkage between operations and finance. Exploring the complex dynamics will likely require simulation and cost modeling.

Measures that Move Companies Forward

As companies have applied the balanced scorecard, we have begun to recognize that the scorecard represents a fundamental change in the underlying assumptions about performance measurement. As the controllers and finance vice presidents involved in the research project took the concept back to their organizations, the project participants found that they could not implement the balanced scorecard without the involvement of the senior managers who have the most complete picture of the company's vision and priorities. This was revealing because most existing performance measurement systems have been designed and overseen by financial experts. Rarely do controllers need to have senior managers so heavily involved.

Probably because traditional measurement systems have sprung from the finance function, the systems have a control bias. That is, traditional performance measurement systems specify the particular actions they want employees to take and then measure to see whether the employees have in fact taken those actions. In that way, the systems try to control behavior. Such measurement systems fit with the engineering mentality of the Industrial Age.

The balanced scorecard, on the other hand, is well suited to the kind of organization many companies are trying to become. The scorecard puts strategy and vision, not control, at the center. It establishes goals but assumes that people will adopt whatever behaviors and take whatever actions are necessary to arrive at those goals. The measures are designed to pull people toward the overall vision. Senior managers may know what the end result should be, but they cannot tell employees exactly how to achieve that result, if only because the conditions in which employees operate are constantly changing.

This new approach to performance measurement is consistent with the initiatives under way in many companies: cross-functional integration, customer-supplier partnerships, global scale, continuous improvement, and team rather than individual accountability. By combining the financial, customer, internal process and innovation, and organizational learning perspectives, the balanced scorecard helps managers understand, at least implicitly, many interrelationships. This understanding can help managers transcend traditional notions about functional barriers and ultimately lead to improved decision making and problem solving. The balanced scorecard keeps companies looking—and moving—forward instead of backward.

Other Measures for the Customer's Perspective

A COMPUTER MANUFACTURER WANTED TO BE THE COMPETITIVE LEADER IN CUSTOMER SATISFACTION, so it measured competitive rankings. The company got the rankings through an outside organization hired to talk directly with customers. The company also wanted to do a better job of solving customers' problems by creating more partnerships with other suppliers. It measured the percentage of revenue from third-party relationships.

The customers of a producer of very expensive medical equipment demanded high reliability. The company developed two customer-based metrics for its operations: equipment up-time percentage and mean-time response to a service call.

A semiconductor company asked each major customer to rank the company against comparable suppliers on efforts to improve quality, delivery time, and price performance. When the manufacturer discovered that it ranked in the middle, managers made improvements that moved the company to the top of customers' rankings.

Other Measures for the Internal Business Perspective

ONE COMPANY RECOGNIZED THAT THE SUCCESS OF ITS TQM PROGRAM DEPENDED ON ALL ITS EMPLOYEES internalizing and acting on the program's messages. The Company performed a monthly survey of 600 randomly selected employees to determine if they were aware of TQM, had changed their behavior because of it, believed the outcome was favorable, or had become missionaries to others.

Hewlett-Packard uses a metric called breakeven time (BET) to measure the effectiveness of its product development cycle. BET measures the time required for all the accumulated expenses in the product and process development cycle (including equipment acquisition) to be recovered by the product's contribution margin (the selling price less manufacturing, delivery, and selling expenses).

A major office products manufacturer, wanting to respond rapidly to changes in the marketplace, set out to reduce cycle time by 50%. Lower levels of the organization aimed to radically cut the times required to process customer orders, order and receive materials from suppliers, move materials and products between plants, produce and assemble products, and deliver products to customers.

How One Company Used a Daily Financial Report to Improve Quality

IN THE 1980s, a chemicals company became committed to a total quality management program and began to make extensive measurements of employee participation, statistical process control, and key quality indicators.[1] Using computerized controls and remote data entry systems, the plant monitored more than 30,000 observations of its production processes every four hours. The department managers and operating personnel who now had access to massive amounts of real- time operational data found their monthly financial reports to be irrelevant.

But one enterprising department manager saw things differently. He created a daily income statement. Each day, he estimated the value of the output from the production process using estimated market prices and subtracted the expenses of raw materials, energy, and capital consumed in the production process. To approximate the cost of producing out-of-conformance product, he cut the revenues from off-spec output by 50% to 100%.

The daily financial report gave operators powerful feedback and motivation and guided their quality and productivity efforts. The department head understood that it is not always possible to improve quality, reduce energy consumption, and increase throughput simultaneously; tradeoffs are usually necessary. He wanted the daily financial statement to guide those tradeoffs. The difference between the input consumed and output produced indicated the success or failure of the employees' efforts on the previous day. The operators were empowered to make decisions that might improve quality, increase productivity, and reduce consumption of energy and materials.

That feedback and empowerment had visible results. When, for example, a hydrogen compressor failed, a supervisor on the midnight shift ordered an emergency repair crew into action. Previously, such a failure of a noncritical component would have been reported in the shift log, where the department manager arriving for work the following morning would have to discover it. The midnight shift supervisor knew the cost of losing of expediting the repairs would be repaid several times over by the output produced by having the compressor back on line before morning.

The department proceeded to set quality and output records. Over time, the department manager became concerned that employees would lose interest in continually improving operations. He tightened the parameters for in-spec production and reset the prices to reflect a 25% premium for output containing only negligible fractions of impurities. The operators continued to improve the production process.

The success of the daily financial report hinged on the manager's ability to establish a financial penalty for what had previously been an intangible variable: the quality of output. With this innovation, it was easy to see where process improvements and capital investments could generate the highest returns.

Notes

1. Source: "Texas Eastman Company," by Robert S. Kaplan, Harvard Business School Case No. 9-190-039.

Originally published in January–February 1992
Reprint 92105

Putting the Balanced Scorecard to Work

ROBERT S. KAPLAN AND DAVID P. NORTON

Executive Summary

IN THEIR GROUND-BREAKING *HARVARD BUSINESS REVIEW* ARTICLE, "The Balanced Scorecard—Measures That Drive Performance" (January–February 1992), Robert Kaplan and David Norton proposed a new measurement system that provided managers with a comprehensive framework to translate a company's strategic objectives into a coherent set of performance measures. Now the authors show how several companies are putting the balanced scorecard to work.

Effective measurement, the authors point out, must be an integral part of the management process. The scorecard complements traditional financial indicators like return-on-investment and operating income with performance measures for customers, internal processes, and innovation and improvement activities. Much more than a measurement exercise, the balanced scorecard is a management system that can motivate breakthrough improvements in such critical areas as product, process, customer, and market development.

Several examples—Rockwater, Apple Computer, and Advanced Micro Devices—illustrate how the scorecard combines measurement and management in different companies. Kaplan and Norton give managers who want to implement their own scorecard some sound, step-by-step advice. Readers are also given a first-hand account of the implementation process in Kaplan's interview with Larry D. Brady, executive vice president of FMC Corporation.

From the experiences of these companies and others, the authors have found that the balanced scorecard is most successful when it is used to drive the process of change.

Today's managers recognize the impact that measures have on performance. But they rarely think of measurement as an essential part of their strategy. For example, executives may introduce new strategies and innovative operating processes intended to achieve breakthrough performance, then continue to use the same short-term financial indicators they have used for decades, measures like return-on-investment, sales growth, and operating income. These managers fail not only to introduce new measures to monitor new goals and processes but also to question whether or not their old measures are relevant to the new initiatives.

Effective measurement, however, must be an integral part of the management process. The balanced scorecard, first proposed in the January–February 1992 issue of *Harvard Business Review* ("The Balanced Scorecard—Measures that Drive Performance," see page 123), provides executives with a comprehensive framework that translates a company's strategic objectives into a coherent set of performance measures. Much more than a measurement exercise, the balanced scorecard is a management system that can motivate breakthrough improvements in such critical areas as product, process, customer, and market development.

The scorecard presents managers with four different perspectives from which to choose measures. It complements traditional financial indicators with measures of performance for customers, internal processes, and innovation and improvement activities. These measures differ from those traditionally used by companies in a few important ways:

Clearly, many companies already have myriad operational and physical measures for local activities. But these local measures are bottom-up and derived from ad hoc processes. The scorecard's measures, on the other hand, are grounded in an organization's strategic objectives and competitive demands. And, by requiring managers to select a limited number of critical indicators within each of the four perspectives, the scorecard helps focus this strategic vision.

In addition, while traditional financial measures report on what happened last period without indicating how managers can improve performance in the next, the scorecard functions as the cornerstone of a company's current and future success.

Moreover, unlike conventional metrics, the information from the four perspectives provides balance between external measures like operating income and internal measures like new product development. This balanced set of measures both reveals the trade-offs that managers have already made among performance measures and encourages them to achieve their goals in the future without making trade-offs among key success factors.

Finally, many companies that are now attempting to implement local improvement programs such as process reengineering, total quality, and employee empowerment lack a sense of integration. The balanced scorecard can serve as the focal point for the organization's efforts, defining and communicating priorities to managers, employees, investors, even customers. As a senior executive at one major company said, "Previously, the one-year budget was our primary management planning device. The balanced scorecard is now used as the language, the benchmark against which all new projects and businesses are evaluated."

The balanced scorecard is not a template that can be applied to businesses in general or even industry-wide. Different market situations, product strategies, and competitive environments require different scorecards. Business units devise customized scorecards to fit their mission, strategy, technology, and culture. In fact, a critical test of a scorecard's success is its transparency: from the 15 to 20 scorecard measures, an observer should be able to see through to the business unit's competitive strategy. A few examples will illustrate how the scorecard uniquely combines management and measurement in different companies.

Rockwater: Responding to a Changing Indusry

Rockwater, a wholly owned subsidiary of Brown & Root/Halliburton, a global engineering and construction company, is a worldwide leader in underwater engineering and construction. Norman Chambers, hired as CEO in late 1989, knew that the industry's competitive world had changed dramatically. "In the 1970s, we were a bunch of guys in wet suits diving off barges into the North Sea with burning torches," Chambers said. But competition in the subsea contracting business had become keener in the 1980s, and many smaller companies left the industry. In addition, the focus of competition had shifted. Several leading oil companies wanted to develop long-term partnerships with their suppliers rather than choose suppliers based on low-price competition.

Rockwater's strategic objectives had to be translated into tangible goals and actions.

With his senior management team, Chambers developed a vision: "As our customers' preferred provider, we shall be the industry leader in providing the highest standards of safety and quality to our clients." He also developed a strategy to implement the vision. The five elements of that strategy were: services that surpass customers' expectations and needs; high levels of customer satisfaction; continuous improvement of safety, equipment reliability, responsiveness, and cost effectiveness; high-quality employees; and realization of shareholder expectations. Those elements were in turn developed into strategic objectives (see the exhibit "Rockwater's

Strategic Objectives"). If, however, the strategic objectives were to create value for the company, they had to
be translated into tangible goals and actions.

Rockwater's senior management team transformed
its vision and strategy into the balanced scorecard's four
sets of performance measures (see the exhibit "Rockwater's Balanced Scorecard"):

Financial Measures: The financial perspective
included three measures of importance to the shareholder. Return-on-capital-employed and cash flow
reflected preferences for short-term results, while forecast reliability signaled the corporate parent's desire to
reduce the historical uncertainty caused by unexpected
variations in performance. Rockwater management
added two financial measures. Project profitability provided focus on the project as the basic unit for planning
and control, and sales backlog helped reduce uncertainty of performance.

Customer Satisfaction: Rockwater wanted to recognize the distinction between its two types of customers:
Tier I customers, oil companies that wanted a high
value-added relationship, and Tier II customers, those
that chose suppliers solely on the basis of price. A price
index, incorporating the best available intelligence on
competitive position, was included to ensure that Rockwater could still retain Tier II customers' business when
required by competitive conditions.

The company's strategy, however, was to emphasize
value-based business. An independent organization conducted an annual survey to rank customers' perceptions
of Rockwater's services compared to those of its competitors. In addition, Tier I customers were asked to supply monthly satisfaction and performance ratings. Rockwater executives felt that implementing these ratings

Rockwater's Strategic Objectives

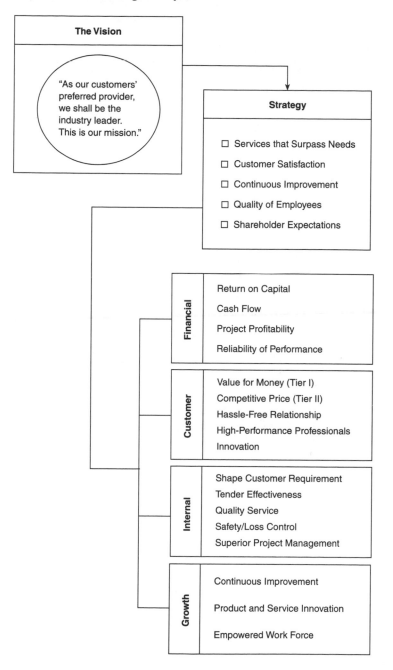

The Vision

"As our customers' preferred provider, we shall be the industry leader. This is our mission."

Strategy

- ☐ Services that Surpass Needs
- ☐ Customer Satisfaction
- ☐ Continuous Improvement
- ☐ Quality of Employees
- ☐ Shareholder Expectations

Financial
Return on Capital
Cash Flow
Project Profitability
Reliability of Performance

Customer
Value for Money (Tier I)
Competitive Price (Tier II)
Hassle-Free Relationship
High-Performance Professionals
Innovation

Internal
Shape Customer Requirement
Tender Effectiveness
Quality Service
Safety/Loss Control
Superior Project Management

Growth
Continuous Improvement
Product and Service Innovation
Empowered Work Force

gave them a direct tie to their customers and a level of market feedback unsurpassed in most industries. Finally, market share by key accounts provided objective evidence that improvements in customer satisfaction were being translated into tangible benefits.

Internal Processes: To develop measures of internal processes, Rockwater executives defined the life cycle of a project from launch (when a customer need was recognized) to completion (when the customer need had been satisfied). Measures were formulated for each of the five business-process phases in this project cycle (see the exhibit "How Rockwater Fulfills Customer Needs"):

Rockwater's Balanced Scorecard

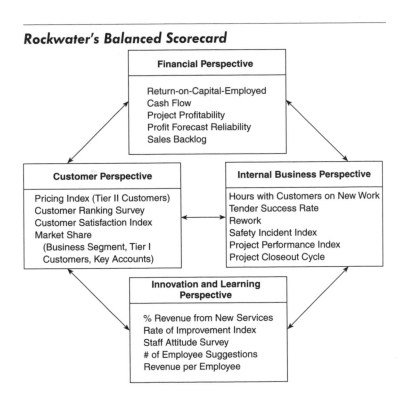

Financial Perspective

Return-on-Capital-Employed
Cash Flow
Project Profitability
Profit Forecast Reliability
Sales Backlog

Customer Perspective

Pricing Index (Tier II Customers)
Customer Ranking Survey
Customer Satisfaction Index
Market Share
  (Business Segment, Tier I
  Customers, Key Accounts)

Internal Business Perspective

Hours with Customers on New Work
Tender Success Rate
Rework
Safety Incident Index
Project Performance Index
Project Closeout Cycle

Innovation and Learning Perspective

% Revenue from New Services
Rate of Improvement Index
Staff Attitude Survey
# of Employee Suggestions
Revenue per Employee

- Identify: number of hours spent with prospects discussing new work;

- Win: tender success rate;

- Prepare and Deliver: project performance effectiveness index, safety/loss control, rework;

- Closeout: length of project closeout cycle.

The internal business measures emphasized a major shift in Rockwater's thinking. Formerly, the company stressed performance for each functional department. The new focus emphasized measures that integrated key business processes. The development of a comprehensive and timely index of project performance effectiveness was viewed as a key core competency for the company. Rockwater felt that safety was also a major competitive factor. Internal studies had revealed that the indirect costs from an accident could be 5 to 50 times the direct costs. The scorecard included a safety index, derived from a comprehensive safety measurement system, that could identify and classify all unde-

Rockwater's executives wanted a metric that would communicate the importance of building relationships with customers.

How Rockwater Fulfills Customer Needs

Customer Need Recognized	#1 Identify	#2 Win	#3 Prepare	#4 Perform	#5 Closeout	Customer Need Met
	Development Cycle		Supply Cycle			

sired events with the potential for harm to people, property, or process.

The Rockwater team deliberated about the choice of metric for the identification stage. It recognized that hours spent with key prospects discussing new work was an input or process measure rather than an output measure. The management team wanted a metric that would clearly communicate to all members of the organization the importance of building relationships with and satisfying customers. The team believed that spending quality time with key customers was a prerequisite for influencing results. This input measure was deliberately chosen to educate employees about the importance of working closely to identify and satisfy customer needs.

Innovation and Improvement: The innovation and learning objectives are intended to drive improvement in financial, customer, and internal process performance. At Rockwater, such improvements came from product and service innovation that would create new sources of revenue and market expansion, as well as from continuous improvement in internal work processes. The first objective was measured by percent revenue from new services and the second objective by a continuous improvement index that represented the rate of improvement of several key operational measures, such as safety and rework. But in order to drive both product/service innovation and operational improvements, a supportive climate of empowered, motivated employees was believed necessary. A staff attitude survey and a metric for the number of employee suggestions measured whether or not such a climate was being created. Finally, revenue per employee measured the outcomes of employee commitment and training programs.

The balanced scorecard has helped Rockwater's management emphasize a process view of operations, motivate its employees, and incorporate client feedback into its operations. It developed a consensus on the necessity of creating partnerships with key customers, the importance of order-of-magnitude reductions in safety-related incidents, and the need for improved management at every phase of multiyear projects. Chambers sees the scorecard as an invaluable tool to help his company ultimately achieve its mission: to be number one in the industry. (See "Building a Balanced Scorecard," on page 176.)

Apple Computer: Adjusting Long-Term Performance

Apple Computer developed a balanced scorecard to focus senior management on a strategy that would expand discussions beyond gross margin, return on equity, and market share. A small steering committee, intimately familiar with the deliberations and strategic thinking of Apple's Executive Management Team, chose to concentrate on measurement categories within each of the four perspectives and to select multiple measurements within each category. For the financial perspective, Apple emphasized shareholder value; for the customer perspective, market share and customer satisfaction; for the internal process perspective, core competencies; and, finally, for the innovation and improvement perspective, employee atti-

Once a technology- and product-focused company, Apple has introduced measures that shift the emphasis toward customers.

tudes. Apple's management stressed these categories in the following order:

Customer Satisfaction: Historically, Apple had been a technology- and product-focused company that competed by designing better computers. Customer satisfaction metrics are just being introduced to orient employees toward becoming a customer-driven company. J.D. Power & Associates, a customer-survey company, now works for the computer industry. However, because it recognized that its customer base was not homogeneous, Apple felt that it had to go beyond J.D. Power & Associates and develop its own independent surveys in order to track its key market segments around the world.

Apple uses the scorecard as a device to plan long-term performance, not as a device to drive operating changes.

Core Competencies: Company executives wanted employees to be highly focused on a few key competencies: for example, user-friendly interfaces, powerful software architectures, and effective distribution systems. However, senior executives recognized that measuring performance along these competency dimensions could be difficult. As a result, the company is currently experimenting with obtaining quantitative measures of these hard-to-measure competencies.

Employee Commitment and Alignment: Apple conducts a comprehensive employee survey in each of its organizations every two years; surveys of randomly selected employees are performed more frequently. The survey questions are concerned with how well employees understand the company's strategy as well as whether or not they are asked to deliver results that are consistent with that strategy. The results of the survey are displayed in terms of both the actual level of employee responses and the overall trend of responses.

Market Share: Achieving a critical threshold of market share was important to senior management not only for the obvious sales growth benefits but also to attract and retain software developers to Apple platforms.

Shareholder Value: Shareholder value is included as a performance indicator, even though this measure is a result—not a driver—of performance. The measure is included to offset the previous emphasis on gross margin and sales growth, measures that ignored the investments required today to generate growth for tomorrow. In contrast, the shareholder value metric quantifies the impact of proposed investments for business creation and development. The majority of Apple's business is organized on a functional basis—sales, product design, and worldwide manufacturing and operations—so shareholder value can be calculated only for the entire company instead of at a decentralized level. The measure, however, helps senior managers in each major organizational unit assess the impact of their activities on the entire company's valuation and evaluate new business ventures.

While these five performance indicators have only recently been developed, they have helped Apple's senior managers focus their strategy in a number of ways. First of all, the balanced scorecard at Apple serves primarily as a planning device, instead of as a control device. To put it another way, Apple uses the measures to adjust the "long wave" of corporate performance, not to drive operating changes. Moreover, the metrics at Apple, with the exception of shareholder value, can be driven both horizontally and vertically into each functional organization. Considered vertically, each individual measure can be broken down into its component parts in order to evaluate how each part contributes to the functioning of the whole. Thought of horizontally, the measures can identify how, for example, design and manufacturing contribute to an area such as customer satisfaction. In addition, Apple has found that its balanced scorecard has helped develop a language of measurable outputs for how to launch and leverage programs.

The five performance indicators at Apple are benchmarked against best-in-class organizations. Today they are used to build business plans and are incorporated into senior executives' compensation plans.

Advanced Micro Devices: Consolidating Strategic Information

Advanced Micro Devices (AMD), a semiconductor company, executed a quick and easy transition to a balanced scorecard. It already had a clearly defined mission, strategy statement, and shared understanding among senior executives about its competitive niche. It also had many performance measures from many different sources and information systems. The balanced scorecard consolidated and focused these diverse measures into a quarterly briefing book that contained seven sections: financial measures; customer-based measures, such as on-time delivery, lead time, and performance-to-schedule; measures of critical business processes in wafer fabrication, assembly and test, new

At Advanced Micro Devices, the scorecard only encapsulated knowledge that managers had already learned.

product development, process technology development (e.g., submicron etching precision), and, finally, measures for corporate quality. In addition, organizational learning was measured by imposing targeted rates of improvements for key operating parameters, such as cycle time and yields by process.

At present, AMD sees its scorecard as a systematic repository for strategic information that facilitates long-term trend analysis for planning and performance evaluation. (See "The Scorecard's Impact on External Reporting," on page 180.)

Driving the Process of Change

The experiences of these companies and others reveal that the balanced scorecard is most successful when it is used to drive the process of change. Rockwater, for instance, came into existence after the merger of two different organizations. Employees came from different cultures, spoke different languages, and had different operating experiences and backgrounds. The balanced scorecard helped the company focus on what it had to do well in order to become the industry leader.

Similarly, Joseph De Feo, chief executive of Service Businesses, one of the three operating divisions of Barclays Bank, had to transform what had been a captive, internal supplier of services into a global competitor. The scorecard highlighted areas where, despite apparent consensus on strategy, there still was considerable disagreement about how to make the strategy operational. With the help of the scorecard, the division eventually achieved consensus concerning the highest priority areas for achievement and improvement and identified additional areas that needed attention, such as quality and productivity. De Feo assessed the impact of the scorecard, saying, "It helped us to drive major change, to become more market oriented, throughout our organization. It provided a shared understanding of our goals and what it took to achieve them."

Analog Devices, a semiconductor company, served as the prototype for the balanced scorecard and now uses it each year to update the targets and goals for division managers. Jerry Fishman, president of Analog, said, "At the beginning, the scorecard drove significant and considerable change. It still does when we focus attention on particular areas, such as the gross margins on new products. But its main impact today is to help sustain programs that our people have been working on for years." Recently, the company has been attempting to integrate the scorecard metrics with *hoshin* planning, a procedure that concentrates an entire company on achieving one or two key objectives each year. Analog's hoshin objectives have included customer service and new product development, for which measures already exist on the company's scorecard.

The scorecard enables managers to see the breadth and totality of company operations.

But the scorecard isn't always the impetus for such dramatic change. For example, AMD's scorecard has yet to have a significant impact because company management didn't use it to drive the change process. Before turning to the scorecard, senior managers had already formulated and gained consensus for the company's mission, strategy, and key performance measures. AMD competes in a single industry segment. The top 12 managers are intimately familiar with the markets, engineering, technology, and other key levers in this segment.

The summary and aggregate information in the scorecard were neither new nor surprising to them. And managers of decentralized production units also already had a significant amount of information about their own operations. The scorecard did enable them to see the breadth and totality of company operations, enhancing their ability to become better managers for the entire company. But, on balance, the scorecard could only encapsulate knowledge that managers in general had already learned.

AMD's limited success with the balanced scorecard demonstrates that the scorecard has its greatest impact when used to drive a change process. Some companies link compensation of senior executives to achieving stretch targets for the scorecard measures. Most are attempting to translate the scorecard into operational measures that become the focus for improvement activities in local units. The scorecard is not just a measurement system; it is a management system to motivate breakthrough competitive performance.

Implementing the Balanced Scorecard at FMC Corporation: An Interview with Larry D. Brady

FMC Corporation is one of the most diversified companies in the United States, producing more than 300 product lines in 21 divisions organized into 5 business segments: industrial chemicals, performance chemicals, precious metals, defense systems, and machinery and equipment. Based in Chicago, FMC has worldwide revenues in excess of $4 billion.

Since 1984, the company has realized annual returns-on-investment of greater than 15%. Coupled with a major recapitalization in 1986, these returns resulted in an increasing shareholder value that significantly exceeded industrial averages. In 1992, the company completed a strategic review to determine the best future course to maximize shareholder value. As a result of that review, FMC adopted a growth strategy to complement its strong operating performance. This strategy required a greater external focus and appreciation of operating trade-offs. To help make the shift, the company decided to use the balanced scorecard. In this interview conducted by Robert S. Kaplan, Larry D. Brady, executive vice president of FMC, talks about the company's experience implementing the scorecard.

Robert S. Kaplan: What's the status of the balanced scorecard at FMC?

Larry D. Brady: Although we are just completing the pilot phase of implementation, I think that the balanced scorecard is likely to become the cornerstone of the management system at FMC. It enables us to translate business unit strategies into a measurement system that meshes with our entire system of management.

For instance, one manager reported that while his division had measured many operating variables in the past, now, because of the scorecard, it had chosen 12 parameters as the key to its strategy implementation. Seven of these strategic variables were entirely new measurements for the division. The manager interpreted this finding as verifying what many other managers were reporting: the scorecard improved the understanding and consistency of strategy implementation. Another manager reported that, unlike monthly financial statements or even his strategic plan, if a rival were to see his scorecard, he would lose his competitive edge.

It's rare to get that much enthusiasm among divisional managers for a corporate initiative. What led you and them to the balanced scorecard?

FMC had a clearly defined mission: to become our customers' most valued supplier. We had initiated many of the popular improvement programs: total quality, managing by objectives, organizational effectiveness, building a high-performance organization. But these efforts had not been effective. Every time we promoted a new program, people in each division would sit back and ask, "How is that supposed to fit in with the six other things we're supposed to be doing?"

"The diversity of initiatives, each with its own slogan, created confusion and mixed signals."

Corporate staff groups were perceived by operating managers as pushing their pet programs on divisions. The diversity of initiatives, each with its own slogan, created confusion and mixed signals about where to concentrate and how the various programs interrelated. At the end of the day, with all these new initiatives, we were still asking division managers to deliver consistent short-term financial performance.

What kinds of measures were you using?

The FMC corporate executive team, like most corporate offices, reviews the financial performance of each operating division monthly. As a highly diversified company that redeploys assets from mature cash generators to divisions with significant growth opportunities, the return-on-capital-employed (ROCE) measure was especially important for us. We were one of the few companies to inflation-adjust our internal financial measures so that we could get a more accurate picture of a division's economic profitability.

At year-end, we rewarded division managers who delivered predictable financial performance. We had run the company tightly for the past 20 years and had been successful. But it was becoming less clear where future growth would come from and where the company should look for breakthroughs into new areas. We had become a high return-on-invest-

"If you're going to ask a division or the corporation to change its strategy, you had better change the system of measurement."

ment company but had less potential for further growth. It was also not at all clear from our financial reports what progress we were making in implementing long-term initiatives. Questions from the corporate office about spending versus budget also reinforced a focus on the short-term and on internal operations.

But the problem went even deeper than that. Think about it. What is the value added of a corporate office that concentrates on making division managers accountable for financial results that can be added up across divisions? We combine a business that's doing well with a business that's doing poorly and have a total business that performs at an average level. Why not split the company up into independent companies and let the market reallocate capital? If we were going to create value by managing a group of diversified companies, we had to understand and provide strategic focus to their operations. We had to be sure that each division had a strategy that would give it sustainable competitive advantage. In addition, we had to be able to assess, through measurement of their operations, whether or not the divisions were meeting their strategic objectives.

If you're going to ask a division or the corporation to change its strategy, you had better change the system of measurement to be consistent with the new strategy.

How did the balanced scorecard emerge as the remedy to the limitations of measuring only short-term financial results?

In early 1992, we assembled a task force to integrate our various corporate initiatives. We wanted to understand what had to be done differently to achieve dramatic improvements in overall organizational effectiveness. We acknowledged that the company may have become too short-term and too internally focused in its business measures. Defining what should replace the financial focus was more difficult. We wanted managers to sustain their search for continuous improvement, but we also wanted them to identify the opportunities for breakthrough performance.

When divisions missed financial targets, the reasons were generally not internal. Typically, division management had inaccurately estimated market demands or had failed to forecast competitive reactions. A new measurement system was needed to lead operating managers beyond achieving internal goals to searching for competitive breakthroughs in the global marketplace. The system would have to focus on measures of customer service, market position, and new products that could generate long-term value for the business. We used the scorecard as the focal point for the discussion. It forced division managers to answer these questions: How do we become our customers' most valued supplier? How do we become more externally focused? What is my division's competitive advantage? What is its competitive vulnerability?

How did you launch the scorecard effort at FMC?

We decided to try a pilot program. We selected six division managers to develop prototype scorecards for their operations. Each division had to perform a strategic analysis to identify its sources of competitive advantage. The 15 to 20 measures in the balanced scorecard had to be organization-specific and had to communicate clearly what short-term measures of operating performance were consistent with a long-term trajectory of strategic success.

Were the six division managers free to develop their own scorecard?

We definitely wanted the division managers to perform their own strategic analysis and to develop their own measures. That was an essential part of creating a consensus between senior and divisional management on operating objectives. Senior management did, however, place some conditions on the outcomes.

First of all, we wanted the measures to be objective and quantifiable. Division managers were to be just as accountable for improving scorecard measures as they had been for using monthly financial reviews. Second, we wanted output measures not process-oriented measures. Many of the improvement programs under way were emphasizing time, quality, and cost measurements. Focusing on T-Q-C measurements, however, encourages managers to seek narrow process improvements instead of breakthrough output targets. Focusing on achieving outputs forces division managers to understand their industry and strategy and help them to quantify strategic success through specific output targets.

Could you illustrate the distinction between process measures and output measures?

You have to understand your industry well to develop the connection between process improvements and outputs achieved. Take three divisional examples of cycle-time measurement, a common process measure.

For much of our defense business, no premium is earned for early delivery. And the contracts allow for reimbursement of inventory holding costs. Therefore, attempts to reduce inventory or cycle times in this business produce no benefit for which the customer is willing to pay. The only benefits from cycle time or inventory reduction occur when reduction in factory-floor complexity leads to real reductions in product cost. The output performance targets must be real cash savings, not reduced inventory levels or cycle times.

In contrast, significant lead-time reductions could be achieved for our packaging machinery business. This improvement led to lower inventory and an option to access an additional 35% of the market. In this case, the cycle-time improvements could be tied to specific targets for increased sales and market share. It wasn't linear, but output seemed to improve each time we improved throughput times.

And in one of our agricultural machinery businesses, orders come within a narrow time window each year. The current build cycle is longer than the ordering window, so all units must be built to the sales forecast. This process of building to forecast leads to high inventory—more than twice the levels of our other businesses—and frequent overstocking and obsolescence of equipment. Incremental reductions in lead time do little to change the economics of this operation. But if the build cycle time could be reduced to less than the six-week ordering time window for part or all of the build schedule, then a break-through occurs. The division can shift to a build-to-order schedule and eliminate the excess inventory caused by building to forecasts. In this case, the benefit from cycle-time reductions is a step-function that comes only when the cycle time drops below a critical level.

So here we have three businesses, three different processes, all of which could have elaborate systems for measuring quality, cost, and time but would feel the impact of improvements in radically different ways. With all the diversity in our business units, senior management really can't have a detailed understanding of the relative impact of time and quality improvements on each unit. All of our senior managers, however, understand output targets, particularly when they are displayed with historical trends and future targets.

Benchmarking has become popular with a lot of companies. Does it tie in to the balanced scorecard measurements?

Unfortunately, benchmarking is one of those initially good ideas that has turned into a fad. About 95% of those companies that have tried benchmarking have spent a lot of money and have gotten very little in return. And the difference between benchmarking and the scorecard helps reinforce the difference between process measures and output measures. It's a lot easier to benchmark a process than to benchmark an output. With the scorecard, we ask each division manager to go outside their organization and determine the approaches that will allow achievement of their long-term output targets. Each of our output measures has an associated long-term target. We have been deliberately vague on specifying when the target is to be accomplished. We want to stimulate a thought process about how to do things differently to achieve the target rather than how to do existing things better. The activity of searching externally for how others have accomplished these breakthrough achievements is called target verification not benchmarking.

Were the division managers able to develop such output-oriented measures?

Well, the division managers did encounter some obstacles. Because of the emphasis on output measures and the previous focus on operations and financial measures, the customer and innovation perspectives proved the most difficult. These were also the two areas where the balanced scorecard process was most helpful in refining and understanding our existing strategies.

But the initial problem was that the management teams ran afoul of both conditions: the measures they proposed tended to be nonquantifiable and input- rather than output-oriented. Several divisions wanted to conduct customer surveys and provide an index of the results. We judged a single index to be of little value and opted instead for harder measures such as price premiums over competitors.

We did conclude, however, that the full customer survey was an excellent vehicle for promoting external focus and, therefore, decided to use survey results to kick-off discussion at our annual operating review

Did you encounter any problems as you launched the six pilot projects?

At first, several divisional managers were less than enthusiastic about the additional freedom they were being given from headquarters. They knew that the heightened visibility and transparency of the scorecard took away the internal trade-offs they had gained experience in making. They initially interpreted the increase in visibility of divisional performance as just the latest attempt by corporate staff to meddle in their internal business processes.

To offset this concern, we designed targets around long-term objectives. We still closely examine the monthly and quarterly statistics, but these statistics now relate to progress in achieving long-term objectives and justify the proper balance between short-term and long-term performance.

We also wanted to transfer quickly the focus from a measurement system to achieving performance results. A measurement orientation reinforces concerns about control and a short-term focus. By emphasizing targets rather than measurements, we could demonstrate our purpose to achieve breakthrough performance.

But the process was not easy. One division manager described his own three-stage implementation process after receiving our directive to build a balanced scorecard: denial—hope it goes away; medicinal—it won't go away, so let's do it quickly and get it over with; ownership—let's do it for ourselves.

In the end, we were successful. We now have six converts who are helping us to spread the message throughout the organization.

I understand that you have started to apply the scorecard not just to operating units but to staff groups as well.

Applying the scorecard approach to staff groups has been even more eye-opening than our initial work with the six operating divisions. We have done very little to define our strategy for corporate staff utilization. I doubt that many companies can respond crisply to the question, "How does staff provide competitive advantage?" Yet we ask that question every day about our line operations. We have just started to ask our staff departments to explain to us whether they are offering low cost or differentiated services. If they are offering neither, we should probably outsource the function. This area is loaded with real potential for organizational development and improved strategic capability.

My conversations with financial people in organizations reveal some concern about the expanded responsibilities implied by developing and maintaining a balanced scorecard. How does the role of the controller change as a company shifts its primary measurement system from a purely financial one to the balanced scorecard?

Historically, we have had two corporate departments involved in overseeing business unit performance. Corporate development was in charge of strategy, and the controller's office kept the historical records and budgeted and measured short-term performance. Strategists came up with five- and ten-year plans, controllers one-year budgets and near-term forecasts. Little interplay occurred between the two groups. But the scorecard now bridges the two. The financial perspective builds on the traditional function performed by controllers. The other three perspectives make the division's long-term strategic objectives measurable.

In our old environment, division managers tried to balance short-term profits with long-term growth, while they were receiving different signals depending on whether or not they were reviewing strategic plans or budgets. This structure did not make the balancing of short-term profits and long-term growth an easy trade-off, and, frankly, it let senior management off the hook when it came to sharing responsibility for making the trade-offs.

Perhaps the corporate controller should take responsibility for all measurement and goal setting, including the systems required to implement these processes. The new corporate controller could be an outstanding system administrator, knowledgeable about the various trade-offs and balances, and skillful in reporting and presenting them. This role does not eliminate the need for strategic planning. It just makes the two systems more compatible. The scorecard can serve to motivate and evaluate performance. But I see its primary value as its ability to join together what had been strong but separated capabilities in strategy development and financial control. It's the operating performance bridge that corporations have never had.

"I see the scorecard as a strategic measurement system, not a measure of our strategy."

How often do you envision reviewing a division's balanced scorecard?

I think we will ask group managers to review a monthly submission from each of their divisions, but the senior corporate team will probably review scorecards quarterly on a rotating basis so that we can review up to seven or eight division scorecards each month.

Isn't it inconsistent to assess a division's strategy on a monthly or quarterly basis? Doesn't such a review emphasize short-term performance?

I see the scorecard as a strategic measurement system, not a measure of our strategy. And I think that's an important distinction. The monthly or quarterly scorecard measures operations that have been configured to be consistent with our long-term strategy.

Here's an example of the interaction between the

short and the long term. We have pushed division managers to choose measures that will require them to create change, for example, penetration of key markets in which we are not currently represented. We can measure that penetration monthly and get valuable short-term information about the ultimate success of our long-term strategy. Of course, some measures, such as annual market share and innovation metrics, don't lend themselves to monthly updates. For the most part, however, the measures are calculated monthly.

Any final thoughts on the scorecard?

I think that it's important for companies not to approach the scorecard as the latest fad. I sense that a number of companies are turning to scorecards in the same way they turned to total quality management, high-performance organization, and so on. You hear about a good idea, several people on corporate staff work on it, probably with some expensive outside consultants, and you put in a system that's a bit different from what existed before. Such systems are only incremental, and you don't gain much additional value from them.

It gets worse if you think of the scorecard as a new measurement system that eventually requires hundreds and thousands of measurements and a big, expensive executive information system. These companies lose sight of the essence of the scorecard: its focus, its simplicity, and its vision. The real benefit comes from making the scorecard the cornerstone of the way you run the business. It should be the core of the management system, not the measurement system. Senior managers alone will determine whether the scorecard becomes a mere record-keeping exercise or the lever to streamline and focus strategy that can lead to breakthrough performance.

Building a Balanced Scorecard

EACH ORGANIZATION IS UNIQUE and so follows its own path for building a balanced scorecard. At Apple and AMD, for instance, a senior finance or business development executive, intimately familiar with the strategic thinking of the top management group, constructed the initial scorecard without extensive deliberations. At Rockwater, however, senior management had yet to define sharply the organization's strategy, much less the key performance levers that drive and measure the strategy's success.

Companies like Rockwater can follow a systematic development plan to create the balanced scorecard and encourage commitment to the scorecard among senior and mid-level managers. What follows is a typical project profile:

1. Preparation

The organization must first define the business unit for which a top-level scorecard is appropriate. In general, a scorecard is appropriate for a business unit that has its own customers, distribution channels, production facilities, and financial performance measures.

2. Interviews: First Round

Each senior manager in the business unit—typically between 6 and 12 executives—receives background material on the balanced scorecard as well as internal documents that describe the company's vision, mission, and strategy.

The balanced scorecard facilitator (either an outside consultant or the company executive who organizes the effort) conducts interviews of approximately 90 minutes each with the senior managers to obtain their input on the company's strategic objectives and tentative proposals for balanced scorecard measures. The facilitator may also interview some principal shareholders to learn about their expectations for the business unit's financial performance, as well as some key customers to learn about their performance expectations for top-ranked suppliers.

3. Executive Workshop: First Round

The top management team is brought together with the facilitator to undergo the process of developing the scorecard (see the exhibit "Begin by Linking Measurements to Strategy"). During the workshop, the group debates the proposed mission and strategy statements until a consensus is reached. The group then moves from the mission and strategy statement to answer the question, "If I succeed with my vision and strategy, how will my performance differ for shareholders; for customers; for internal business processes; for my ability to innovate, grow, and improve?"

Videotapes of interviews with shareholder and customer representatives can be shown to provide an external perspective to the deliberations. After defining the key success factors, the group formulates a preliminary balanced scorecard containing operational measures for the strategic objectives. Frequently, the group proposes far more than four or five measures for each perspective. At this time, narrowing the choices is not critical, though straw votes can be taken to see whether or not some of the proposed measures are viewed as low priority by the group.

Begin by Linking Measurements to Strategy

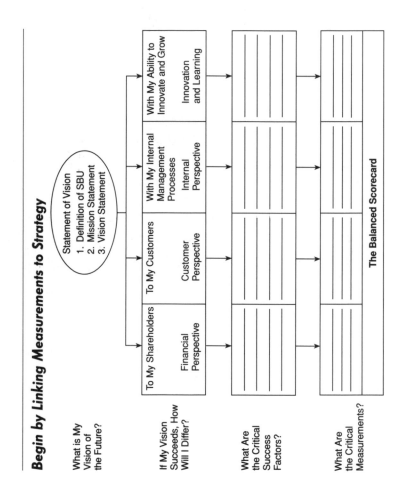

4. Interviews: Second Round

The facilitator reviews, consolidates, and documents the output from the executive workshop and interviews each senior executive about the tentative balanced scorecard. The facilitator also seeks opinions about issues involved in implementing the scorecard.

5. Executive Workshop: Second Round

A second workshop, involving the senior management team, their direct subordinates, and a larger number of middle managers, debates the organization's vision, strategy statements, and the tentative scorecard. The participants, working in groups, comment on the proposed measures, link the various change programs under way to the measures, and start to develop an implementation plan. At the end of the workshop, participants are asked to formulate stretch objectives for each of the proposed measures, including targeted rates of improvement.

6. Executive Workshop: Third Round

The senior executive team meets to come to a final consensus on the vision, objectives, and measurements developed in the first two workshops; to develop stretch targets for each measure on the scorecard; and to identify preliminary action programs to achieve the targets. The team must agree on an implementation program, including communicating the scorecard to employees, integrating the scorecard into a management philosophy, and developing an information system to support the scorecard.

7. Implementation

A newly formed team develops an implementation plan for the scorecard, including linking the measures to databases and information systems, communicating the balanced scorecard throughout the organization, and encouraging and facilitating the development of second-level metrics for decentralized units. As a result of this process, for instance, an entirely new executive information system that links top-level business unit metrics down through shop floor and site-specific operational measures could be developed.

8. Periodic Reviews

Each quarter or month, a blue book of information on the balanced scorecard measures is prepared for both top management review and discussion with managers of decentralized divisions and departments. The balanced scorecard metrics are revisited annually as part of the strategic planning, goal setting, and resource allocation processes.

The Scorecard's Impact on External Reporting

SEVERAL MANAGERS HAVE ASKED whether or not the balanced scorecard is applicable to external reporting. If the scorecard is indeed a driver of long-term performance, shouldn't this information be relevant to the investment community?

In fact, the scorecard does not translate easily to the investment community. A scorecard makes sense primarily for business units and divisions with a well-defined strategy. Most companies have several divisions, each with its own mission and strategy, whose scorecards cannot be aggregated into an overall corporate scorecard. And if the scorecard does indeed provide a transparent vision into a unit's strategy, then the information, even the measures being used, might be highly sensitive data that could reveal much of value to competitors. But most important, as a relatively recent innovation, the scorecard would benefit from several years of experimentation within companies before it becomes a systematic part of reporting to external constituencies.

Even if the scorecard itself were better suited to external reporting, at present the financial community itself shows little interest in making the change from financial to strategic reporting. One company president has found the outside financial community leery of the principles that ground the scorecard: "We use the scorecard more with our customers than with our investors. The financial community is skeptical about long-term indicators and occasionally tells us about some empirical evidence of a negative correlation between stock prices and attention to total quality and internal processes."

However, the investment community has begun to focus on some key metrics of new product performance. Could this be an early sign of a shift to strategic thinking?

Originally published in September–October 1993
Reprint 93505

Using the Balanced Scorecard as a Strategic Management System

ROBERT S. KAPLAN AND DAVID P. NORTON

Executive Summary

AS COMPANIES TRANSFORM THEMSELVES TO COM-PETE in the world of information, their ability to exploit intangible assets is becoming more decisive than their ability to manage physical assets. Several years ago, Robert S. Kaplan and David P. Norton introduced the *balanced scorecard*, which supplemented traditional financial measures with criteria that measured perform-ance from the perspectives of customers, internal busi-ness processes, and learning and growth. The score-card enabled companies to track financial results while monitoring progress in building the capabilities they would need for growth.

Recently, some companies have gone further and dis-covered the scorecard's value as the cornerstone of a new strategic management system. Traditional manage-ment systems rely on financial measures, which bear little relation to progress in achieving long-term strategic objectives. The scorecard introduces four new processes that help companies connect long-term objectives with short-term actions.

The first—*translating the vision*—helps managers build a consensus around the company's strategy and express it in terms that can guide action at the local level. The second—*communicating and linking*—lets managers communicate their strategy up and down the organization and link it to unit and individual goals. The third—*business planning*—enables companies to integrate their business and financial plans. The fourth—*feedback and learning*—gives companies the capacity for strategic learning, which consists of gathering feedback, testing the hypotheses on which strategy was based, and making the necessary adjustments.

As COMPANIES AROUND THE WORLD TRANS-FORM THEMSELVES for competition that is based on information, their ability to exploit intangible assets has become far more decisive than their ability to invest in and manage physical assets. Several years ago, in recognition of this change, we introduced a concept we called the *balanced scorecard*. The balanced scorecard supplemented traditional financial measures with criteria that measured performance from three additional perspectives—those of customers, internal business processes, and learning and growth. (See the exhibit "Translating Vision and

Lofty vision and strategy statements don't translate easily into action at the local level.

Strategy: Four Perspectives.") It therefore enabled companies to track financial results while simultaneously monitoring progress in building the capabilities and acquiring the intangible assets they would need for future growth. The scorecard wasn't a replacement for financial measures; it was their complement.

Recently, we have seen some companies move beyond our early vision for the scorecard to discover its value as the cornerstone of a new strategic management system. Used this way, the scorecard addresses a serious deficiency in traditional management systems: their inability to link a company's long-term strategy with its short-term actions.

Most companies' operational and management control systems are built around financial measures and targets, which bear little relation to the company's progress in achieving long-term strategic objectives. Thus the emphasis most companies place on short-term financial measures leaves a gap between the development of a strategy and its implementation.

Managers using the balanced scorecard do not have to rely on short-term financial measures as the sole indicators of the company's performance. The scorecard lets them introduce four new management processes that, separately and in combination, contribute to linking long-term strategic objectives with short-term actions. (See the exhibit "Managing Strategy: Four Processes.")

The first new process—*translating the vision*—helps managers build a consensus around the organization's vision and strategy. Despite the best intentions of those at the top, lofty statements about becoming "best in class," "the number one supplier," or an "empowered organization" don't translate easily into operational terms that provide useful guides to action at the local

Translating Vision and Strategy: Four Perspectives

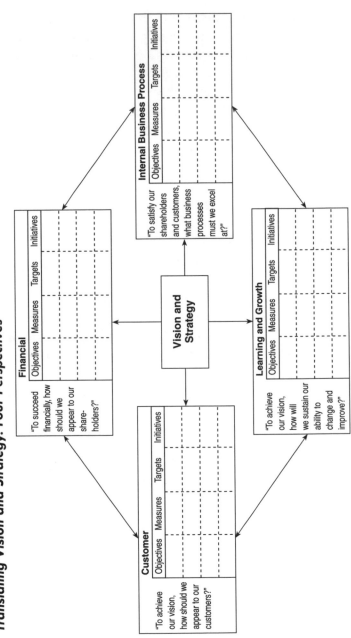

level. For people to act on the words in vision and strategy statements, those statements must be expressed as an integrated set of objectives and measures, agreed upon by all senior executives, that describe the long-term drivers of success.

The second process—*communicating and linking*—lets managers communicate their strategy up and down the organization and link it to departmental and individual objectives. Traditionally, departments are evaluated by their financial performance, and individual incentives are tied to short-term financial goals. The scorecard gives managers a way of ensuring that all levels of the organization understand the long-term strat-

Managing Strategy: Four Processes

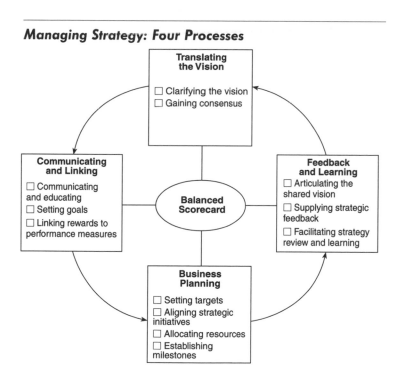

egy and that both departmental and individual objectives are aligned with it.

The third process—*business planning*—enables companies to integrate their business and financial plans. Almost all organizations today are implementing a variety of change programs, each with its own champions, gurus, and consultants, and each competing for senior executives' time, energy, and resources. Managers find it difficult to integrate those diverse initiatives to achieve their strategic goals—a situation that leads to frequent disappointments with the programs' results. But when managers use the ambitious goals set for balanced scorecard measures as the basis for allocating resources and setting priorities, they can undertake and coordinate only those initiatives that move them toward their long-term strategic objectives.

The fourth process—*feedback and learning*—gives companies the capacity for what we call strategic learning. Existing feedback and review processes focus on whether the company, its departments, or its individual employees have met their budgeted financial goals. With the balanced scorecard at the center of its management systems, a company can monitor short-term results from the three additional perspectives—customers, internal business processes, and learning and growth—and evaluate strategy in the light of recent performance. The scorecard thus enables companies to modify strategies to reflect real-time learning.

None of the more than 100 organizations that we have studied or with which we have worked implemented their first balanced scorecard with the intention of developing a new strategic management system. But in each one, the senior executives discovered that the scorecard supplied a framework and thus a focus for many critical management processes: departmental and individual goal setting, business planning, capital allocations, strategic initiatives, and feedback and learning. Previously, those processes were uncoordinated and often directed at short-term operational goals. By building the scorecard, the senior executives started a process of change that has gone well beyond the original idea of simply broadening the company's performance measures.

For example, one insurance company—let's call it National Insurance—developed its first balanced scorecard to create a new vision for itself as an underwriting specialist. But once National started to use it, the scorecard allowed the CEO and the senior management team not only to introduce a new strategy for the organization but also to overhaul the company's management system. The CEO subsequently told employees in a letter addressed to the whole organization that National would thenceforth use the balanced scorecard and the philosophy that it represented to manage the business.

National built its new strategic management system step-by-step over 30 months, with each step representing an incremental improvement. (See the exhibit "How One Company Built a Strategic Management System.") The iterative sequence of actions enabled the company to reconsider each of the four new management processes two or three times before the system stabilized and became an established part of National's overall management system. Thus the CEO was able to transform the company so that everyone could focus on achieving long-term strategic objectives—something that no purely financial framework could do.

Translating the Vision

The CEO of an engineering construction company, after working with his senior management team for several months to develop a mission statement, got a phone call from a project manager in the field. "I want you to

---

How One Company Built a Strategic Management System

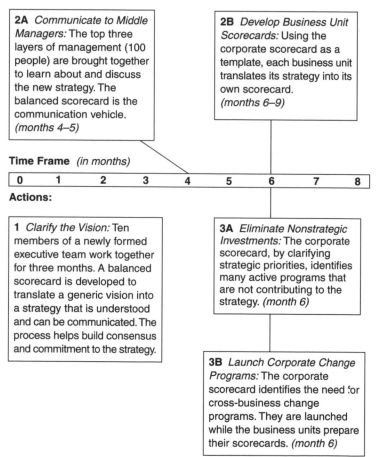

2A *Communicate to Middle Managers:* The top three layers of management (100 people) are brought together to learn about and discuss the new strategy. The balanced scorecard is the communication vehicle. *(months 4–5)*

2B *Develop Business Unit Scorecards:* Using the corporate scorecard as a template, each business unit translates its strategy into its own scorecard. *(months 6–9)*

Time Frame *(in months)*

| 0 | 1 | 2 | 3 | 4 | 5 | 6 | 7 | 8 |

Actions:

1 *Clarify the Vision:* Ten members of a newly formed executive team work together for three months. A balanced scorecard is developed to translate a generic vision into a strategy that is understood and can be communicated. The process helps build consensus and commitment to the strategy.

3A *Eliminate Nonstrategic Investments:* The corporate scorecard, by clarifying strategic priorities, identifies many active programs that are not contributing to the strategy. *(month 6)*

3B *Launch Corporate Change Programs:* The corporate scorecard identifies the need for cross-business change programs. They are launched while the business units prepare their scorecards. *(month 6)*

know," the distraught manager said, "that I believe in the mission statement. I want to act in accordance with the mission statement. I'm here with my customer. What am I supposed to do?"

The mission statement, like those of many other organizations, had declared an intention to "use high-

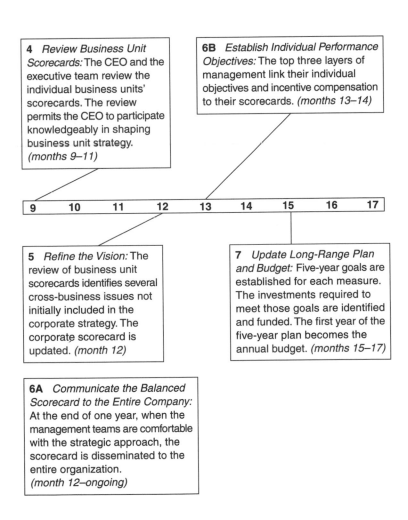

4 *Review Business Unit Scorecards:* The CEO and the executive team review the individual business units' scorecards. The review permits the CEO to participate knowledgeably in shaping business unit strategy. *(months 9–11)*

6B *Establish Individual Performance Objectives:* The top three layers of management link their individual objectives and incentive compensation to their scorecards. *(months 13–14)*

| 9 | 10 | 11 | 12 | 13 | 14 | 15 | 16 | 17 |

5 *Refine the Vision:* The review of business unit scorecards identifies several cross-business issues not initially included in the corporate strategy. The corporate scorecard is updated. *(month 12)*

7 *Update Long-Range Plan and Budget:* Five-year goals are established for each measure. The investments required to meet those goals are identified and funded. The first year of the five-year plan becomes the annual budget. *(months 15–17)*

6A *Communicate the Balanced Scorecard to the Entire Company:* At the end of one year, when the management teams are comfortable with the strategic approach, the scorecard is disseminated to the entire organization. *(month 12–ongoing)*

quality employees to provide services that surpass customers' needs." But the project manager in the field with his employees and his customer did not know how to translate those words into the appropriate actions. The phone call convinced the CEO that a large gap existed between the mission statement and employees' knowl-

---

How One Company Built a Strategic Management System (continued)

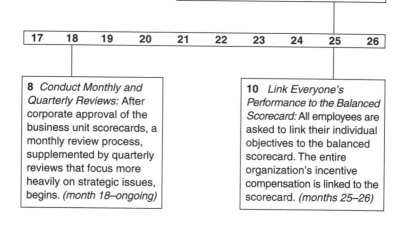

9 *Conduct Annual Strategy Review:* At the start of the third year, the initial strategy has been achieved and the corporate strategy requires updating. The executive committee lists ten strategic issues. Each business unit is asked to develop a position on each issue as a prelude to updating its strategy and scorecard. *(months 25–26)*

| 17 | 18 | 19 | 20 | 21 | 22 | 23 | 24 | 25 | 26 |

8 *Conduct Monthly and Quarterly Reviews:* After corporate approval of the business unit scorecards, a monthly review process, supplemented by quarterly reviews that focus more heavily on strategic issues, begins. *(month 18–ongoing)*

10 *Link Everyone's Performance to the Balanced Scorecard:* All employees are asked to link their individual objectives to the balanced scorecard. The entire organization's incentive compensation is linked to the scorecard. *(months 25–26)*

Note: Steps 7, 8, 9, and 10 are performed on a regular schedule. The balanced scorecard is now a routine part of the management process.

edge of how their day-to-day actions could contribute to realizing the company's vision.

Metro Bank (not its real name), the result of a merger of two competitors, encountered a similar gap while building its balanced scorecard. The senior executive group thought it had reached agreement on the new organization's overall strategy: "to provide superior service to targeted customers." Research had revealed five basic market segments among existing and potential customers, each with different needs. While formulating the measures for the customer-perspective portion of their balanced scorecard, however, it became apparent that although the 25 senior executives agreed on the

The Balanced Scorecard

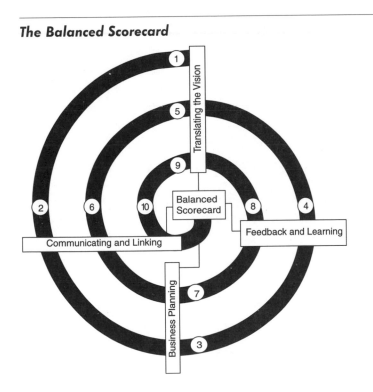

words of the strategy, each one had a different definition of *superior service* and a different image of the *targeted customers.*

The exercise of developing operational measures for the four perspectives on the bank's scorecard forced the 25 executives to clarify the meaning of the strategy statement. Ultimately, they agreed to stimulate revenue growth through new products and services and also agreed on the three most desirable customer segments. They developed scorecard measures for the specific products and services that should be delivered to customers in the targeted segments as well as for the relationship the bank should build with customers in each segment. The scorecard also highlighted gaps in employees' skills and in information systems that the bank would have to close in order to deliver the selected value propositions to the targeted customers. Thus, creating a balanced scorecard forced the bank's senior managers to arrive at a consensus and then to translate their vision into terms that had meaning to the people who would realize the vision.

Communicating and Linking

"The top ten people in the business now understand the strategy better than ever before. It's too bad," a senior executive of a major oil company complained, "that we can't put this in a bottle so that everyone could share it." With the balanced scorecard, he can.

One company we have worked with deliberately involved three layers of management in the creation of its balanced scorecard. The senior executive group formulated the financial and customer objectives. It then mobilized the talent and information in the next two levels of managers by having them formulate the internal-business-process and learning-and-growth objectives that would drive the achievement of the financial and customer goals. For example, knowing the importance of satisfying customers' expectations of on-time delivery, the broader group identified several internal business processes—such as order processing, scheduling, and fulfillment—in which the company had to excel. To do so, the company would have to retrain frontline employees and improve the information systems available to them. The group developed performance measures for those critical processes and for staff and systems capabilities.

Broad participation in creating a scorecard takes longer, but it offers several advantages: Information from a larger number of managers is incorporated into the internal objectives; the managers gain a better understanding of the company's long-term strategic goals; and such broad participation builds a stronger commitment to achieving those goals. But getting managers to buy into the scorecard is only a first step in linking individual actions to corporate goals.

The balanced scorecard signals to everyone what the organization is trying to achieve for shareholders and customers alike. But to align employees' individual performances with the overall strategy, scorecard users generally engage in three activities: communicating and educating, setting goals, and linking rewards to performance measures.

COMMUNICATING AND EDUCATING

Implementing a strategy begins with educating those who have to execute it. Whereas some organizations opt to hold their strategy close to the vest, most believe that they should disseminate it from top to bottom. A broad-based communication program shares with all employees the strategy and the critical objectives they have to meet if the strategy is to succeed. Onetime events such as the distribution of brochures or newsletters and the holding of "town meetings" might kick off the program. Some organizations post bulletin boards that illustrate and explain the balanced scorecard measures, then update them with monthly results. Others use group-ware and electronic bulletin boards to distribute the scorecard to the desktops of all employees and to encourage dialogue about the measures. The same media allow employees to make suggestions for achieving or exceeding the targets.

The balanced scorecard, as the embodiment of business unit strategy, should also be communicated upward in the organization—to corporate headquarters and to the corporate board of directors. With the scorecard, business units can quantify and communicate their long-term strategies to senior executives using a comprehensive set of linked financial and nonfinancial measures. Such communication informs the executives and the board in specific terms that long-term strategies designed for competitive success are in place. The measures also provide the basis for feedback and accountability. Meeting short-term financial targets should not constitute satisfactory performance when other measures indicate that the long-term strategy is either not working or not being implemented well.

Should the balanced scorecard be communicated beyond the boardroom to external shareholders? We believe that as senior executives gain confidence in the ability of the scorecard measures to monitor strategic performance and predict future financial performance, they will find ways to inform outside investors about those measures without disclosing competitively sensitive information.

Skandia, an insurance and financial services company based in Sweden, issues a supplement to its annual report called "The Business Navigator"—"an instrument to help us navigate into the future and thereby stimulate renewal and development." The supplement describes Skandia's strategy and the strategic measures the company uses to communicate and evaluate the strategy. It also provides a report on the company's performance along those measures during the year. The measures are customized for each operating unit and include, for example, market share, customer satisfaction and retention, employee competence, employee empowerment, and technology deployment.

The personal scorecard helps to communicate corporate and unit objectives to the people and teams performing the work.

Communicating the balanced scorecard promotes commitment and accountability to the business's long-term strategy. As one executive at Metro Bank declared, "The balanced scorecard is both motivating and obligating."

SETTING GOALS

Mere awareness of corporate goals, however, is not enough to change many people's behavior. Somehow, the organization's high-level strategic objectives and measures must be translated into objectives and measures for operating units and individuals.

The exploration group of a large oil company developed a technique to enable and encourage individuals to set goals for themselves that were consistent with the organization's. It created a small, fold-up personal scorecard that people could carry in their shirt pockets or wallets. (See the exhibit "The Personal Scorecard.") The scorecard contains three levels of information. The first describes corporate objectives, measures, and targets. The second leaves room for translating corporate targets into targets for each business unit. For the third level, the company asks both individuals and teams to articulate which of their own objectives would be consistent with the business unit and corporate objectives, as well as what initiatives they would take to achieve their objectives. It also asks them to define up to five performance measures for their objectives and to set targets for each measure. The personal scorecard helps to communicate corporate and business unit objectives to the people and teams performing the work, enabling them to translate the objectives into meaningful tasks and targets for themselves. It also lets them keep that information close at hand—in their pockets.

LINKING REWARDS TO PERFORMANCE MEASURES

Should compensation systems be linked to balanced scorecard measures? Some companies, believing that tying financial compensation to performance is a powerful lever, have moved quickly to establish such a linkage. For example, an oil company that we'll call Pioneer Petroleum uses its scorecard as the sole basis for computing incentive compensation. The company ties 60% of its executives' bonuses to their achievement of ambi-

The Personal Scorecard

Corporate Objectives

☐ Double our corporate value in seven years.
☐ Increase our earnings by an average of 20% per year.
☐ Achieve an internal rate of return 2% above the cost of capital.
☐ Increase both production and reserves by 20% in the next decade.

Corporate Targets					Scorecard Measures	Business Unit Targets					Team/Individual Objectives and Initiatives
1995	1996	1997	1998	1999		1995	1996	1997	1998	1999	
					Financial						1.
100	120	160	180	250	Earnings (in millions of dollars)						
100	450	200	210	225	Net cash flow						
100	85	80	75	70	Overhead and operating expenses						2.
					Operating						
100	75	73	70	64	Production costs per barrel						
100	97	93	90	82	Development costs per barrel						3.
100	105	108	108	110	Total annual production						

Team/Individual Measures	Targets						
1.							4.
2.							
3.							
4.							5.
5.							

Name:

Location:

tious targets for a weighted average of four financial indicators: return on capital, profitability, cash flow, and operating cost. It bases the remaining 40% on indicators of customer satisfaction, dealer satisfaction, employee satisfaction, and environmental responsibility (such as a percentage change in the level of emissions to water and air). Pioneer's CEO says that linking compensation to the scorecard has helped to align the company with its strategy. "I know of no competitor," he says, "who has this degree of alignment. It is producing results for us."

As attractive and as powerful as such linkage is, it nonetheless carries risks. For instance, does the company have the right measures on the scorecard? Does it have valid and reliable data for the selected measures? Could unintended or unexpected consequences arise from the way the targets for the measures are achieved? Those are questions that companies should ask.

Furthermore, companies traditionally handle multiple objectives in a compensation formula by assigning weights to each objective and calculating incentive compensation by the extent to which each weighted objective was achieved. This practice permits substantial incentive compensation to be paid if the business unit overachieves on a few objectives even if it falls far short on others. A better approach would be to establish minimum threshold levels for a critical subset of the strategic measures. Individuals would earn no incentive compensation if performance in a given period fell short of any threshold. This requirement should motivate people to achieve a more balanced performance across short- and long-term objectives.

Some organizations, however, have reduced their emphasis on short-term, formula-based incentive systems as a result of introducing the balanced scorecard. They have discovered that dialogue among executives and managers about the scorecard—both the formulation of the measures and objectives and the explanation of actual versus targeted results—provides a better opportunity to observe managers' performance and abilities. Increased knowledge of their managers' abilities makes it easier for executives to set incentive rewards subjectively and to defend those subjective evaluations—a process that is less susceptible to the game playing and distortions associated with explicit, formula-based rules.

One company we have studied takes an intermediate position. It bases bonuses for business unit managers on two equally weighted criteria: their achievement of a financial objective—economic value added—over a three-year period and a subjective assessment of their performance on measures drawn from the customer, internal-business-process, and learning-and-growth perspectives of the balanced scorecard.

That the balanced scorecard has a role to play in the determination of incentive compensation is not in doubt. Precisely what that role should be will become clearer as more companies experiment with linking rewards to scorecard measures.

Business Planning

"Where the rubber meets the sky": That's how one senior executive describes his company's long-range-planning process. He might have said the same of many other companies because their financially based management systems fail to link change programs and resource allocation to long-term strategic priorities.

The problem is that most organizations have separate procedures and organizational units for strategic planning and for resource allocation and budgeting. To formulate their strategic plans, senior executives go off-site annually and engage for several days in active discussions facilitated by senior planning and development managers or external consultants. The outcome of this exercise is a strategic plan articulating where the company expects (or hopes or prays) to be in three, five, and ten years. Typically, such plans then sit on executives' bookshelves for the next 12 months.

Meanwhile, a separate resource-allocation and budgeting process run by the finance staff sets financial targets for revenues, expenses, profits, and investments for the next fiscal year. The budget it produces consists almost entirely of financial numbers that generally bear little relation to the targets in the strategic plan.

Which document do corporate managers discuss in their monthly and quarterly meetings during the following year? Usually only the budget, because the periodic reviews focus on a comparison of actual and budgeted results for every line item. When is the strategic plan next discussed? Probably during the next annual off-site meeting, when the senior managers draw up a new set of three-, five-, and ten-year plans.

Building a scorecard enables a company to link its financial budgets with its strategic goals.

The very exercise of creating a balanced scorecard forces companies to integrate their strategic planning and budgeting processes and therefore helps to ensure that their budgets support their strategies. Scorecard users select measures of progress from all four scorecard perspectives and set targets for each of them. Then they determine which actions will drive them toward their targets, identify the measures they will apply to those drivers from the four perspectives, and establish the short-term milestones that will mark their progress along the strategic paths they have selected. Building a scorecard thus enables a company to link its financial budgets with its strategic goals.

For example, one division of the Style Company (not its real name) committed to achieving a seemingly impossible goal articulated by the CEO: to double revenues in five years. The forecasts built into the organization's existing strategic plan fell $1 billion short of this objective. The division's managers, after considering various scenarios, agreed to specific increases in five different performance drivers: the number of new stores opened, the number of new customers attracted into new and existing stores, the percentage of shoppers in each store converted into actual purchasers, the portion of existing customers retained, and average sales per customer.

By helping to define the key drivers of revenue growth and by committing to targets for each of them, the division's managers eventually grew comfortable with the CEO's ambitious goal.

The process of building a balanced scorecard—clarifying the strategic objectives and then identifying the few critical drivers—also creates a framework for managing an organization's various change programs. These initiatives—reengineering, employee empowerment, time-based management, and total quality management, among others—promise to deliver results but also compete with one another for scarce resources, including the scarcest resource of all: senior managers' time and attention.

Shortly after the merger that created it, Metro Bank, for example, launched more than 70 different initiatives. The initiatives were intended to produce a more competitive and successful institution, but they were inadequately integrated into the overall strategy. After building their balanced scorecard, Metro Bank's managers dropped many of those programs—such as a marketing effort directed at individuals with very high net worth—and consolidated others into initiatives that were better aligned with the company's strategic objectives. For example, the managers replaced a program aimed at enhancing existing low-level selling skills with a major initiative aimed at retraining salespersons to become trusted financial advisers, capable of selling a broad range of newly introduced products to the three selected customer segments. The bank made both changes because the scorecard enabled it to gain a better understanding of the programs required to achieve its strategic objectives.

Once the strategy is defined and the drivers are identified, the scorecard influences managers to concentrate on improving or reengineering those processes most critical to the organization's strategic success. That is how the scorecard most clearly links and aligns action with strategy.

The final step in linking strategy to actions is to establish specific short-term targets, or milestones, for the balanced scorecard measures. Milestones are tangible expressions of managers' beliefs about when and to what degree their current programs will affect those measures.

In establishing milestones, managers are expanding the traditional budgeting process to incorporate strategic as well as financial goals. Detailed financial planning remains important, but financial goals taken by themselves ignore the three other balanced scorecard perspectives. In an integrated planning and budgeting process, executives continue to budget for short-term financial performance, but they also introduce short-term targets for measures in the customer, internal-business-process, and learning-and-growth perspectives. With those milestones established, managers can continually test both the theory underlying the strategy and the strategy's implementation.

At the end of the business planning process, managers should have set targets for the long-term objectives they would like to achieve in all four scorecard perspectives; they should have identified the strategic initiatives required and allocated the necessary resources to those initiatives; and they should have established milestones for the measures that mark progress toward achieving their strategic goals.

Feedback and Learning

"With the balanced scorecard," a CEO of an engineering company told us, "I can continually test my strategy. It's like performing real-time research." That is exactly the capability that the scorecard should give senior managers: the ability to know at any point in its implementation whether the strategy they have formulated is, in fact, working, and if not, why.

The first three management processes—translating the vision, communicating and linking, and business planning—are vital for implementing strategy, but they are not sufficient in an unpredictable world. Together they form an important single-loop-learning process—single-loop in the sense that the objective remains constant, and any departure from the planned trajectory is seen as a defect to be remedied. This single-loop process does not require or even facilitate reexamination of either the strategy or the techniques used to implement it in light of current conditions.

Most companies today operate in a turbulent environment with complex strategies that, though valid when they were launched, may lose their validity as business conditions change. In this kind of environment, where new threats and opportunities arise constantly, companies must become capable of what Chris Argyris calls *double-loop learning*—learning that produces a change in people's assumptions and theories about cause-and-effect relationships. (See "Teaching Smart People How to Learn," *Harvard Business Review* May–June 1991.)

Budget reviews and other financially based management tools cannot engage senior executives in double-loop learning—first, because these tools address performance from only one perspective, and second, because they don't involve strategic learning. Strategic learning consists of gathering feedback, testing the hypotheses on which strategy was based, and making the necessary adjustments.

The balanced scorecard supplies three elements that are essential to strategic learning. First, it articulates the company's shared vision, defining in clear and operational terms the results that the company, as a team, is trying to achieve. The scorecard communicates a holistic model that links individual efforts and accomplishments to business unit objectives.

Second, the scorecard supplies the essential strategic feedback system. A business strategy can be viewed as a set of hypotheses about cause-and-effect relationships.

A strategic feedback system should be able to test, validate, and modify the hypotheses embedded in a business unit's strategy. By establishing short-term goals, or milestones, within the business planning process, executives are forecasting the relationship between changes in performance drivers and the associated changes in one or more specified goals. For example, executives at Metro Bank estimated the amount of time it would take for improvements in training and in the availability of information systems before employees could sell multiple financial products effectively to existing and new customers. They also estimated how great the effect of that selling capability would be.

Another organization attempted to validate its hypothesized cause-and-effect relationships in the balanced scorecard by measuring the strength of the linkages among measures in the different perspectives. (See the exhibit "How One Company Linked Measures from the Four Perspectives.") The company found significant correlations between employees' morale, a measure in the learning-and-growth perspective, and customer satisfaction, an important customer perspective measure. Customer satisfaction, in turn, was correlated with faster payment of invoices—a relationship that led to a substantial reduction in accounts receivable and hence a higher return on capital employed. The company also found correlations between employees' morale and the number of suggestions made by employees (two learning-and-growth measures) as well as between an increased number of suggestions and lower rework (an internal-business-process measure). Evidence of such strong correlations help to confirm the organization's business strategy. If, however, the expected correlations are not found over time, it should be an indication to executives that the theory underlying the unit's strategy may not be working as they had anticipated.

Especially in large organizations, accumulating sufficient data to document significant correlations and causation among balanced scorecard measures can take a

How One Company Linked Measures from the Four Perspectives

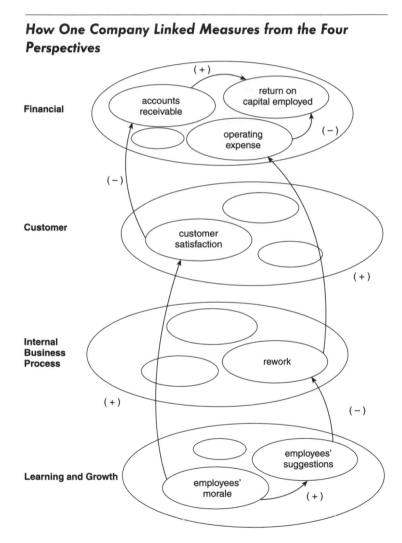

long time—months or years. Over the short term, managers' assessment of strategic impact may have to rest on subjective and qualitative judgments. Eventually, however, as more evidence accumulates, organizations may be able to provide more objectively grounded estimates of cause-and-effect relationships. But just getting managers to think systematically about the assumptions underlying their strategy is an improvement over the current practice of making decisions based on short-term operational results.

Third, the scorecard facilitates the strategy review that is essential to strategic learning. Traditionally, companies use the monthly or quarterly meetings between corporate and division executives to analyze the most recent period's financial results. Discussions focus on past performance and on explanations of why financial objectives were not achieved. The balanced scorecard, with its specification of the causal relationships between performance drivers and objectives, allows corporate and business unit executives to use their periodic review sessions to evaluate the validity of the unit's strategy and the quality of its execution. If the unit's employees and managers have delivered on the performance drivers (retraining of employees, availability of information systems, and new financial products and services, for instance), then their failure to achieve the expected outcomes (higher sales to targeted customers, for example) signals that the theory underlying the strategy may not be valid. The disappointing sales figures are an early warning.

Managers should take such disconfirming evidence seriously and reconsider their shared conclusions about market conditions, customer value propositions, competitors' behavior, and internal capabilities. The result of

such a review may be a decision to reaffirm their belief
in the current strategy but to adjust the quantitative
relationship among the strategic measures on the balanced scorecard. But they also might conclude that the
unit needs a different strategy (an example of double-
loop learning) in light of new knowledge about market
conditions and internal capabilities. In any case, the
scorecard will have stimulated key executives to learn
about the viability of their strategy. This capacity for
enabling organizational learning at the executive level—
strategic learning—is what distinguishes the balanced
scorecard, making it invaluable for those who wish to
create a strategic management system.

Toward a New Strategic Management System

Many companies adopted early balanced-scorecard concepts to improve their performance measurement systems. They achieved tangible but narrow results.
Adopting those concepts provided clarification, consensus, and focus on the desired improvements in performance. More recently, we have seen companies expand
their use of the balanced scorecard, employing it as the
foundation of an integrated and iterative strategic management system. Companies are using the scorecard to

- clarify and update strategy,

- communicate strategy throughout the company,

- align unit and individual goals with the strategy,

- link strategic objectives to long-term targets and
  annual budgets,

- identify and align strategic initiatives, and

- conduct periodic performance reviews to learn about and improve strategy.

The balanced scorecard enables a company to align its management processes and focuses the entire organization on implementing long-term strategy. At National Insurance, the scorecard provided the CEO and his managers with a central framework around which they could redesign each piece of the company's management system. And because of the cause-and-effect linkages inherent in the scorecard framework, changes in one component of the system reinforced earlier changes made elsewhere. Therefore, every change made over the 30-month period added to the momentum that kept the organization moving forward in the agreed-upon direction.

Without a balanced scorecard, most organizations are unable to achieve a similar consistency of vision and action as they attempt to change direction and introduce new strategies and processes. The balanced scorecard provides a framework for managing the implementation of strategy while also allowing the strategy itself to evolve in response to changes in the company's competitive, market, and technological environments.

Originally published in January–February 1996
Reprint 96107

About the Contributors

THOMAS G. CUCUZZA is a partner with Price Waterhouse's Financial and Cost Management practice, based in Cleveland, Ohio. He specializes in the design and development of advanced cost management systems. In 1989, Mr. Cucuzza designed and developed one of the first generation software tools for implementing activity-based costing (ABC). In 1994, he designed Price Waterhouse's ACTIVA software, a client-server-based cost management system, which is used throughout the world. He is currently designing a state-of-the-art ABC software solution for an automotive manufacturer. In addition, he has implemented profitability reporting, performance measurement, and cost management systems for numerous clients in the manufacturing and service sector.

ANTONIO DÁVILA is assistant professor of business administration at IESE, the International Graduate School of Management of the University of Navarra (Spain). He has published articles on cost accounting and performance measurement. His recent research focuses on the design of formal systems in new product development. Currently, he is studying how companies use management control systems to implement strategy and has written several cases on the topic.

PETER F. DRUCKER is a writer, teacher, and consultant whose twenty-nine books have been published in more than twenty languages. He is the founder of the Peter F. Drucker Foundation for Nonprofit Management and has counseled numerous governments, public service institutions, and major corporations.

ROBERT G. ECCLES is a founder and president of Advisory Capital Partners, Inc. (ACP). ACP provides a broad range of advisory services to large and medium sized corporations in the areas of strategy, organizational design and culture, and financial structure. Prior to starting ACP, Dr. Eccles was a professor at Harvard Business School and chairman of the Organizational Behavior and Human Resources Management Area. He is the author of a number of articles and books, including *Beyond the Hype: Rediscovering the Essence of Management* (HBS Press, 1994) and *Doing Deals: Investment Banks at Work* (HBS Press, 1988).

ROBERT S. KAPLAN is the Marvin Bower Professor of Leadership Development at the Harvard Business School. His research, teaching, and consulting focus on new cost and performance measurement systems, primarily activity-based costing and the balanced scorecard. He has authored or coauthored more than one hundred papers and nine books. His recent books include, *Cost and Effect: Using Integrated Cost Systems to Drive Profitability and Performance* (HBS Press, 1998), with Robin Cooper, and *The Balanced Scorecard: Translating Strategy into Action* (HBS Press, 1996) with David Norton. In 1994, HBS Management Productions produced his four-part videotape series, "Measuring Corporate Performance," which presents concepts and companies' experiences with activity-based cost management and the balanced scorecard.

CHRISTOPHER MEYER, PH.D., is the managing principal of Integral, Inc., a management consulting firm specializing in strategy, technology, and innovation management. He is the author of *Fast Cycle Time and Relentless Growth*. He is an instructor at the California Institute of Technology Industrial Relations Center and former academic director of Stanford's Fast Cycle Strategy Program.

JOSEPH A. NESS is a partner with Price Waterhouse's Financial and Cost Management practice, based in St. Louis, Missouri. He has over twenty years experience in the design and implementation of profitability, performance, and cost management systems with clients throughout the manufacturing and service sector. Mr. Ness recently led an international effort to develop Price Waterhouse's activity-based cost management software product ACTIVA. He is currently responsible for overseeing its implementation at two *Fortune* 500 companies and a large federal agency.

DAVID P. NORTON is the founder and president of Renaissance Wordwide Strategy Group, an international consulting firm specializing in business strategy, performance measurement, and organizational renewal. He has authored numerous works, including three *Harvard Business Review* articles, and is a contributing columnist for the *Journal of Strategic Performance Management*. He is the coauthor with Dr. Robert Kaplan of *The Balanced Scorecard: Translating Strategy into Action* (HBS Press, 1996). Mr. Norton is a frequent lecturer, and his work with the balanced scorecard has been the subject of many articles and professional conferences.

ROBERT SIMONS is the Charles M. Williams Professor of Business Administration at Harvard Business School, and director of the school's Division of Research. He has served as a consultant to a number of corporations on matters of strategic control and performance measurement. Mr. Simons is the author of *Levers of Control: How Managers Use Innova-*

tive Control Systems to Drive Strategic Renewal (HBS Press, 1995). His ongoing research into the relationship between business strategy and management control systems has been published in books as well as journals such as *Harvard Business Review, Strategic Management Journal, and Accounting and Management.*

Index

Knowledge is Power.
(So don't forget to recharge.)

For e-mail updates on powerful new business ideas
and management issues, sign up for the *Harvard Business
Review* listserv at **www.hbsp.harvard.edu.**

For ideas any time keep the Harvard Business School
Publishing Web page in mind.

○ Access more than 7,500 articles, books, case studies, videos
  and CD-ROMs by leaders in management practice.
○ Search by author, key word, and more.
○ Order on-line and download *Harvard Business Review*
  articles any time.

Visit **www.hbsp.harvard.edu**, or call **(800) 668-6780**
or **(617) 496-1449.**

 Harvard Business School Publishing
The power of ideas at work.